D0712196

[1908]

New Poems:
THE OTHER PART

Rainer Maria Rilke

Translated by Edward Snow

North Point Press · San Francisco · 1987

Translation copyright © 1987 by Edward Snow
Printed in the United States of America
Library of Congress Catalogue Card Number: 86-62835
ISBN: 0-86547-271-8

Contents

Introduction

Rilke sent the finished manuscript of *New Poems: The Other Part* (*Der neuen Gedichte anderer Teil*) to his publisher on 17 August 1908, less than a year after completing the original *New Poems* (*Neue Gedichte*), and scarcely eight months after the first volume's December 1907 publication. All ninety-nine of the poems in the second volume (one hundred and six, if one counts the poems that form sequences) were composed between one August and the next, and in periods of sustained creative output even more intense than those that produced the first volume: forty poems in August 1907 alone, followed by another forty-six in the summer of 1908. The two volumes thus issue virtually uninterrupted from the same initial impulse. And they pursue the same "new" project: to subordinate lyric "expression" to workmanlike "making" ("not feelings," Rilke wrote in retrospect, "but things I had felt") and achieve in poetry the same objective, free standing integrity Rilke admired in Rodin's sculpture and Cézanne's painting, his constant touchstones during this period:

> Somehow I too must come to make things; not plastic, but written things—*realities* that emerge from handwork. Somehow I too must discover the smallest basic element, the cell of *my* art, the tangible immaterial means of representation for everything. . . .[1]

Given, then, all that the two volumes have in common, it seems inevitable that the boundary between them should by

1. Letter to Lou Andreas-Salome, 10 August 1903. For a more elaborate account of Rilke's project, see my introduction to *New Poems (1907)*, North Point Press, 1984.

now have virtually disappeared: we routinely refer to the poems of both as the *New Poems*, and at most distinguish them as parts one and two of a single work. Yet when Rilke sent the manuscript of the companion volume to his publisher, what he stressed was its separateness and distance from the original work:

> As I arranged the poems, I had the impression that the new volume could quite suitably join up with the earlier one: the course is almost parallel—only somewhat higher, it seems to me, and at a greater depth and with more distance. If the third volume is to join these two, a similar intensification will still have to be achieved in the ever more objective mastering of reality, out of which, entirely of its own accord, the wider significance and clearer validity of all things arises.[2]

It is hard to know what to make of language so general and abstract, but close attention to *New Poems: The Other Part* everywhere confirms its difference. Its mood and personality are so different, in fact, from the 1907 *New Poems* as to make it feel "other" in the same nontrivial sense that both volumes feel "new." This is nowhere truer than in the poems with explicit parallels in the first volume. "Archaic Torso of Apollo," for instance, announces *New Poems: The Other Part* in the same way that "Early Apollo" begins the original *New Poems*. But in making this connection it creates a virtual paradigm for how the second volume will "intensify" and differ from the first:

EARLY APOLLO [1907]

As sometimes between still leafless branches
a morning looks through that is already
radiant with spring: so nothing in his head
could obstruct the splendor of all poems

from striking us with almost lethal force;
for there is still no shadow in his gaze,
still too cool for laurel are his temples,
and only later from his eyebrows' arches

will the rose garden lift up tall-stemmed,
from which petals, each alone, released
will drift down upon the mouth's trembling,

2. Letter to Anton Kippenberg, 18 August 1908.

which now is yet quiet, never-used and gleaming
and only drinking something with its smile
as though its song were being infused in him.

ARCHAIC TORSO OF APOLLO [1908]

We never knew his head and all the light
that ripened in his fabled eyes. But
his torso still glows like a candelabra,
in which his gazing, turned down low,

holds fast and shines. Otherwise the surge
of the breast could not blind you, nor a smile
run through the slight twist of the loins
toward that center where procreation thrived.

Otherwise this stone would stand deformed and curt
under the shoulders' invisible plunge
and not glisten just like wild beasts' fur;

and not burst forth from all its contours
like a star: for there is no place
that does not see you. You must change your life.

Both poems present the sculptural object as a first gesture,
and the task of description as an intense imaginative project.
And in both one can feel Rilke handling line and syntax as
"materials" out of which to sculpt contours and build torques
and tensions. But beyond this it is mainly the differences that
register. "Archaic Torso of Apollo" has a drive and a weight
that make "Early Apollo" seem almost coy and languorous by
comparison. Its language is richer and more impacted, and
pursues its course with almost reckless daring. Assonance and
alliteration are pushed to near-limits in the pursuit of a dense
internal music. "Unerhörtes Haupt" is typical, especially in its
rhyme with "zurückgeschraubt." A similar impacting occurs
at the level of image. "Kandelaber" can mean either "cande-
labra" or "gas lamp," and this visual choice is woven into the
subsequent texture of the poem, becoming explicit in the con-
trast between the solitary standing presence of line 9 and the
glittering beast's pelt of line 11, and condensing again in the
ambiguous "durchsichtigem Sturz" of line 10, which can con-
jure up (among other things) either the glittering cascade of a

waterfall or the airless drop of a bell jar. "Zurückgeschraubt" itself epitomizes the poem's daring. It refers to the candela-bra/gas lamp's "lowered" light, but by way of a metonymic, elliptical allusion to the "screwing back" of a control knob. The disconcerting, almost ruthless kinesis of the idea (rein-forced by the very sound of the word) informs our sense of how tenaciously the gaze inwardly endures. It also forges a link with the poem's own turnings, and with the "slight twist of the loins" that in line 8 leads to the fertile center.

"Zurückgeschraubt," in fact, could describe in general the difference between the poems in the two volumes. Those in the second tend, like "Archaic Torso," to feel indrawn and "screwed tighter" in relation to those in the first. Grammar and syntax become more convoluted and prolonged, and at the same time move faster. An inner momentum bordering on the compulsive often hurtles the reader through a poem—sometimes toward a breaking point, as in "Night Drive," sometimes toward a final, unexpected reversal, as in "Archaic Torso" or "Black Cat," and sometimes, as in "Comforting of Elijah," going out of control. This intensification is a matter of content as well as texture. The object of description in "Early Apollo" more or less passively accepts the metaphors it elicits; they embellish it (however brilliantly) as their ground, their occasion. But the metaphors of "Archaic Torso" inhere fiercely in their object, as if they were the very principle of its being. One can feel something of the same difference in many of the finest companion poems, "The Steps of the Orangery" (1907) and "Roman Campagna" (1908), for instance, or "Procession of the Virgin" (1907) and "Easter Eve" (1908), or the "Buddha" poems in both volumes. It is even true when the "objects" describe themselves, as in "The Courtesan" (1907) and "The Lute" (1908):

THE COURTESAN [1907]

Venice's sun will in my hair
prepare a gold: all alchemy's
illustrious issue. My brows, which
are like her bridges, look at how

they arch the soundless danger
of my eyes, which keep a secret commerce
with her canals, so that the sea
rises and falls and changes in them. Who

saw me once is envious of my dog,
since often on him in distracted pauses
my hand, not ever charred on any heat,

invulnerable and bejeweled, rests—.
And boys, the hopes of ancient houses,
perish at my mouth as if by poison.

THE LUTE [1908]

I am the lute. If you wish to describe
my body, with its beautiful arching stripes:
speak of me as you would of a ripe
full-bodied fig. Exaggerate

the darkness that you see in me. It was
Tullia's darkness. In her most private place
there wasn't so much, and her bright hair
was like a light-filled hall. Sometimes

she took some sound from my surface
into her face and sang while I played.
then I tensed myself against her yielding,
until at last my inmost self was in her.

"The Courtesan" is a wonderful mood-piece, and something of a tour de force in its evocation of Carpaccio's Venice. But one is never really tempted to hear the voice as more than a conceit. No "real" courtesan speaks in the poem, and not much otherness of any kind interferes with our pleasure in image and rhythm. Even the sexuality and the seductiveness are very much surface gestures. But in "The Lute" the object *exists*, and the voice of the poem fully belongs to it. The narcissism, the self-possession, the combination of frankness and disregard, the absorption in distant memories, all are elements of a powerful inwardness, and help define the lute in its tantalizing inaccessibility. The sexuality in the poem, though less stressed, seems more immediate and real, largely because it is conceived in terms of tensions that inhere in the poem's own address. Yielding and resistance, invitation and evasion, isolation and intimate relation, unguarded surfaces and sought-for depths, these compose the lute's relation to both "Tullia" and the poet/reader, and give the poem a charged separateness that "The Courtesan" lacks. The brilliant reversal in the final lines, where the sex of the lute seems to change, and the narcissistic object of admiration turns into an avatar of sexual straining and release, dictates an entirely new set of terms to the reader, who is left suspended between sensations of consummation and escape.

Such tropes become more common in the second volume, as what draws the self takes on the power to question, displace, evade, estrange, undo, or otherwise disrupt it. The interpenetration of object and consciousness is in *New Poems* mainly a visionary theme: there is a euphoric sense of "re-seeing" the world in ways that transcend the opposition between inner and outer, empty and fulfilled. But *New Poems: The Other Part* seeks out darker, more problematical versions of that relation. The bull in "Corrida" is "from all eternity" *gegen* the matador he "recognizes," where *gegen* means "toward," "against," and "in relation to" all at once. The young Don Juan feels an involuntary "inclination" toward a passing woman from whom "a strange ancient image" bars him. "Encounter in the Chestnut Avenue" describes a coming-nearer of the distantly glimpsed object, which, as consummated image, leaves the observer more isolated than before:

> But suddenly the shade was deep,
> and nearby eyes lay gazing
>
> from a clear new unselfconscious face,
> which, as in a portrait, lived intensely
> in the instant things split off again:
> first there forever, and then not at all.

Many of the most striking poems—"The Beggars," "Foreign Family," "The Site of the Fire," "Corpse-Washing," and "Snake-Charming," for example—construct relation out of estrangement; *fremd* (foreign, alien, strange) is the word that appears over and over again. "Foreign" figures compel recognition, and draw the viewer with a combination of fascination and dread. The seductiveness of "One of the Old Women" is an especially vivid, Baudelairean instance:

In the evenings sometimes (you know how it feels?)
when they suddenly stop and nod backwards
and show you from under their half-hats
a smile that seems made of patches . . .

Next to them then is a building,
endless, and they lure you along
with the riddle of their scabs,
with the hat, the shawl, and the walk.

With the hand, which under the collar's nape
waits in secret and longs for you:
as if it wished to wrap your hands
in a scrap of picked-up paper.

Against these uncanny figures with their "pull" on the viewer are the figures of enduring isolation that "pull in" around grief, pain, deprivation, and disfigurement, as with the urns that close "The Pavilion":

How little has been driven off:
everything still knows, still weeps, still causes pain—.
And as you walk away through the tear-damp
unfrequented avenue

for a long time you feel on the roof's ledge
those urns standing there, cold and split apart:
yet determined still to hold together
around the ashes of old aches.

Rilke's ambiguity makes "split" (*zerspalten*) describe both the individual urns and their connection with one another. Holding on here, to grief and to the "pangs" of an interred life, becomes a means of cohering, a way of keeping both relation and the place of feeling alive. This theme, though less apparent than some of the others in *New Poems: The Other Part*, may ultimately go deepest. "Archaic Torso of Apollo," "The Leper King," "The Blind Man," "Portrait," "The Pavilion," and

"The Coat of Arms" all work variations on it. In place of *über-steigen*, "to transcend," we tend to get *überstehen*, with its un-translatable combination of "to endure," "to live through," and "to survive." What makes the theme so rich is the way this pulling in and hardening around severance and loss tends to grasp the vital core. Holding back and grim endurance become centers of emanation, and move toward exaltation and grace. This is true of the archaic torso's radiant bursting-forth, the self-abandoned blind man's "marriage," the "contagious-ness" of the leper king's "new dignity," and the winged exfoli-ations of the coat of arms's "indrawnness." "Persian Helio-trope" provides a gentle paradigm: as "sweet words" there "at night in sentences/pull close together, refusing separation," they "perfume forth" to fill the silent four-poster that contains them. The last two poems in the volume consummate this theme beautifully, first with the cradled sleep of the ancient beetle-stones, then with the unattached Buddha installed in glory, welcomed as "center of all centers, core of cores." But its most powerful expression is "The Solitary," where the de-structive element—here conceived of as *distances*—drives aloneness further and further into bliss:

> No: a tower shall rise out of my heart,
> and I myself will be placed at its edge;
> where nothing else exists, once again pain
> and unsayableness, once again world.
>
> Still one thing alone in immensity
> growing dark and then light again,
> still one last face full of longing
> thrust out into the unappeasable,
>
> still one uttermost face made of stone
> heeding only its own inner gravity,
> while the distances that silently destroy it
> force it on to an ever deeper bliss.

•

The gains of *New Poems: The Other Part*, however, are not without their costs. If it is more "intense" than *New Poems*, it is also less varied and relaxed. In its drive toward objectivity it loses the youthful quality of the first volume, and this registers as real loss. The gentle wistfulness of "Portrait of My Father as a Young Man" or "The Carousel"—itself supremely assured—scarcely survives into the second volume. Nor does the first volume's extraordinary openness to the realm of women. In spite of isolated examples like "Woman in Love," there is nothing in *The Other Part* to compare with the series of voicings of female desire that launches the erotic theme in *New Poems*. Nor, in spite of poems like "Lady at a Mirror" and "The Rose-Interior," is there anything like the feeling for feminine withinness and apartness that produces the original volume's magnificent concluding poems.

If *New Poems* sometimes flirts with sentimentality and false ingenuousness, *The Other Part* can seem near-pathological in its pursuit of "hardness." Under the guise of maker ("not feelings but things I had felt") Rilke sometimes seems to be cultivating distance for its own sake, and trying to expunge feeling itself. "Corrida" is a good example. It is a brilliant poem, technically and thematically, and it works out the relationship between its two antagonists with impeccable balance. But a coldness infuses its very making. The indifference that it cultivates even acquires a kind of sadistic edge, as in the queasy sexuality of its ending:

> before he serenely, unspitefully,
> leaning on himself, calmly, carelessly
> into that great wave, turned round and once more
> rolling toward him, above its lost thrust
> almost gently sinks his sword.

Finally, it must be said that too often the poems in *The Other Part* seem *merely* willed, as if the desire to repeat the first volume were without any deep impulse or intuition. This is especially true of the early poems that stretch from "Dolphins" through "Magnificat." Here important poems are almost ruined by a piling up of alliteration and assonance for their own sake, as in "Dolphins," "The Last Judgment," and "The

Temptation." Other times elaborate wordplay and rhyme schemes attempt to compensate for impoverished content, as in "The King of Münster" and the wretched "Absalom's Rebellion," surely one of the worst poems Rilke ever wrote. And few of the seemingly endless biblical poems ever acquire a life of their own. It is not until "Adam" and "Eve" that Rilke truly finds his voice and his themes, and after that the poetry rises to a level of sustained accomplishment comparable to that of the original *New Poems*. It would be a shame if the reader were deterred by those mediocre first poems. For what follows—especially "Adam" through "The Lute"—though not the greatest, is probably the most consistently *fascinating* run of poems in all of Rilke. If there is such a thing as an "unknown Rilke," it is probably in *New Poems: The Other Part* that it waits to be discovered.

•

I would like again to express my gratitude to other translators of Rilke: the selections of Stephen Mitchell, M.D. Herter Norton, C. F. MacIntyre, Robert Bly, and Franz Wright have all aided me at one time or another—as, of course, has J. B. Leishman's translation of the complete *New Poems*. I would also like to thank the friends who have been so generous with their comments: Albert Cook, Alan Grob, Ed Hirsch, Philip Lopate, Scott McLean, Stephen Mitchell, Michael Winkler, and Bill Zavatsky have all provided helpful suggestions. And I owe a special debt of thanks to Winnie Hamilton. She has been a constant critic, sounding board, and arbiter during the latter stages of these translations. Whatever success I may have achieved would have been impossible without her patience and generosity.

New Poems [1908]
THE OTHER PART

A mon grand Ami Auguste Rodin

Archaïscher Torso Apollos

Wir kannten nicht sein unerhörtes Haupt,
darin die Augenäpfel reiften. Aber
sein Torso glüht noch wie ein Kandelaber,
in dem sein Schauen, nur zurückgeschraubt,

sich hält und glänzt. Sonst könnte nicht der Bug
der Brust dich blenden, und im leisen Drehen
der Lenden könnte nicht ein Lächeln gehen
zu jener Mitte, die die Zeugung trug.

Sonst stünde dieser Stein entstellt und kurz
unter der Schultern durchsichtigem Sturz
und flimmerte nicht so wie Raubtierfelle;

und bräche nicht aus allen seinen Rändern
aus wie ein Stern: denn da is keine Stelle,
die dich nicht sieht. Du mußt dein Leben ändern.

Archaic Torso of Apollo

We never knew his head and all the light
that ripened in his fabled eyes. But
his torso still glows like a candelabra,
in which his gazing, turned down low,

holds fast and shines. Otherwise the surge
of the breast could not blind you, nor a smile
run through the slight twist of the loins
toward that center where procreation thrived.

Otherwise this stone would stand deformed and curt
under the shoulders' invisible plunge
and not glisten just like wild beasts' fur;

and not burst forth from all its contours
like a star: for there is no place
that does not see you. You must change your life.

Kretische Artemis

Wind der Vorgebirge: war nicht ihre
Stirne wie ein lichter Gegenstand?
Glatter Gegenwind der leichten Tiere,
formtest du sie: ihr Gewand

bildend an die unbewußten Brüste
wie ein wechselvolles Vorgefühl?
Während sie, als ob sie alles wüßte,
auf das Fernste zu, geschürzt und kühl,

stürmte mit den Nymphen und den Hunden,
ihren Bogen probend, eingebunden
in den harten hohen Gurt;

manchmal nur aus fremden Siedelungen
angerufen und erzürnt bezwungen
von dem Schreien um Geburt.

Cretan Artemis

Wind of the foothills: was her brow not
like some bright obstruction?
Unruffled head wind of the swiftest beasts:
did *you* shape her, molding

her garment to the unconscious breasts
like a change-filled premonition?
While she, as if she knew everything,
fixed on the farthest point, cool and kilted,

stormed with the nymphs and the hunting dogs,
testing her bow, bound tightly
in the high unbending girth;

only now and then from distant outposts
called to and angrily overmastered
by the screaming out for birth.

Artemis, virgin huntress and warrior, ancient Greek goddess of both chastity
and childbirth. "Cretan" suggests an untamed, pre-Hellenic youthfulness,
pairing her perhaps (sister to brother) with the "archaic" Apollo of the pre-
vious poem.

Leda

Als ihn der Gott in seiner Not betrat,
erschrak er fast, den Schwan so schön zu finden;
er ließ sich ganz verwirrt in ihm verschwinden.
Schon aber trug ihn sein Betrug zur Tat,

bevor er noch des unerprobten Seins
Gefühle prüfte. Und die Aufgetane
erkannte schon den Kommenden im Schwane
und wußte schon: er bat um Eins,

das sie, verwirrt in ihrem Widerstand,
nicht mehr verbergen konnte. Er kam nieder
und halsend durch die immer schwächre Hand

ließ sich der Gott in die Geliebte los.
Dann erst empfand er glücklich sein Gefieder
und wurde wirklich Schwan in ihrem Schooß.

Leda

When the god in his great need crossed inside,
he was shocked almost to find the swan so beautiful;
he slipped himself inside it all confused.
But his deceit bore him toward the deed

before he'd put that untried being's
feelings to the test. And the opened woman
saw at once who was coming in the swan
and understood: he asked *one* thing

which she, confused in her resistance,
no longer could hold back. The god came down
and necking through the ever weaker hand

released himself into the one he loved.
Then only he felt his feathers with delight,
and grew truly swan within her womb.

Delphine

Jene Wirklichen, die ihrem Gleichen
überall zu wachsen und zu wohnen
gaben, fühlten an verwandten Zeichen
Gleiche in den aufgelösten Reichen,
die der Gott, mit triefenden Tritonen,
überströmt bisweilen übersteigt;
denn da hatte sich das Tier gezeigt:
anders als die stumme, stumpfgemute
Zucht der Fische, Blut von ihrem Blute
und von fern dem Menschlichen geneigt.

Eine Schar kam, die sich überschlug,
froh, als fühlte sie die Fluten glänzend:
Warme, Zugetane, deren Zug
wie mit Zuversicht die Fahrt bekränzend,
leichtgebunden um den runden Bug
wie um einer Vase Rumpf und Rundung,
selig, sorglos, sicher vor Verwundung,
aufgerichtet, hingerissen, rauschend
und im Tauchen mit den Wellen tauschend
die Trireme heiter weitertrug.

Und der Schiffer nahm den neugewährten
Freund in seine einsame Gefahr
und ersann für ihn, für den Gefährten,
dankbar eine Welt und hielt für wahr,
daß er Töne liebte, Götter, Gärten
und das tiefe, stille Sternenjahr.

Dolphins

Those real ones, who gave their equal
the power to grow and to take hold
everywhere, felt through kindred signs
equivalences in the fluid realm
which the god, with drenching Tritons,
inundated sometimes surmounts;
for there the animal had shown itself:
different from the mute, phlegmatic
stock of fishes, alive with *their* blood
and drawn to the human from afar.

A band of them came up, somersaulting,
gay, as though they felt the waters sparkling:
warm, deep-feeling beings, whose convoy,
wreathing the voyage as if with confidence,
lightly joined around the curving bow
as if circling a vase's midriff,
blissful, carefree, secure from being wounded,
catapulted up, swept away, surging
and in dives exchanging with the waves,
bore the trireme brightly after it.

And the sailor took this newly given friend
into his lonely peril and gratefully
devised for it, for the companion there,
a world, and knew beyond all doubt
that it too loved music, gods, gardens,
and the deep, silent stellar year.

l. 1, *Jene Wirklichen*: presumably the ancient Greeks, with their twin passions
for reality and mythological world-making.
l. 5, *Tritons*: lesser sea deities (half man, half fish) of Greek mythology.
l. 20, *trireme*: an ancient Greek warship or galley with three tiers of oars.

Die Insel der Sirenen

Wenn er denen, die ihm gastlich waren,
spät, nach ihrem Tage noch, da sie
fragten nach den Fahrten und Gefahren,
still berichtete: er wußte nie,

wie sie schrecken und mit welchem jähen
Wort sie wenden, daß sie so wie er
in dem blau gestillten Inselmeer
die Vergoldung jener Inseln sähen,

deren Anblick macht, daß die Gefahr
umschlägt; denn nun ist sie nicht im Tosen
und im Wüten, wo sie immer war.
Lautlos kommt sie über die Matrosen,

welche wissen, daß es dort auf jenen
goldnen Inseln manchmal singt—,
und sich blindlings in die Ruder lehnen,
wie umringt

von der Stille, die die ganze Weite
in sich hat und an die Ohren weht,
so als wäre ihre andre Seite
der Gesang, dem keiner widersteht.

The Island of the Sirens

When he began, his hosts still gathered there,
late, well past their day, since they
inquired about the journeys and the perils,
to quietly tell it: he never knew

how to frighten them and with just which sudden
phrase to turn them, so that like him they
would gaze into that blue stilled island-sea
and see the gilding of those islands

whose sight makes peril suddenly
reverse; for now it isn't in the raging
and the fury, where it always was.
Soundlessly it steals upon the sailors,

who know that out there on those
golden islands sometimes there is a singing—,
and blindly lean into the oars,
as though ringed in

by the quiet, which has the whole expanse
within itself and blows uncannily
upon the ears, as though its other side
were the song that no one can resist.

Klage um Antinous

Keiner begriff mir von euch den bithynischen Knaben
(daß ihr den Strom anfaßtet und von ihm hübt . . .).
Ich verwöhnte ihn zwar. Und dennoch: wir haben
ihn nur mit Schwere erfüllt und für immer getrübt.

Wer vermag denn zu lieben? Wer kann es?—Noch keiner.
Und so hab ich unendliches Weh getan—.
Nun ist er am Nil der stillenden Götter einer,
und ich weiß kaum welcher und kann ihm nicht nahn.

Und ihr warfet ihn noch, Wahnsinnige, bis in die Sterne,
damit ich euch rufe und dränge: meint ihr den?
Was ist er nicht einfach ein Toter. Er wäre es gerne.
Und vielleicht wäre ihm nichts geschehn.

Lament for Antinous

Not one of you could grasp the Bithynian boy
(that you might seize the stream and lift it from him . . .).
I pampered him it's true. And yet: we have
only filled him with heaviness and forever dimmed him.

Who is able then to love? Who knows how? —None as yet.
And so I have inflicted endless pain—.
Now he is among the Nile's pacifying gods,
and I scarcely know which and can't get close to him.

And still you would hurl him, madmen, into the stars,
that I might call on you and urge: do you mean *that* one?
Why is he not just someone dead. He'd like it fine.
And perhaps nothing would have happened to him.

Antinous, young favorite of the Roman emperor Hadrian (A.D. 76–138),
drowned while the imperial barge was sailing up the Nile. His death was
"clouded" almost from the beginning: it may have been an accident or a sui-
cide or an obscure sacrifice. The historical Hadrian (unlike the reluctant
speaker of Rilke's poem) responded with extravagant acts of mourning,
founding the city of Antinoupolis where Antinous drowned, setting up stat-
ues of the youth throughout the empire (over 300 representations are
known), and crediting his mages' and courtiers' theory that the new star he
claimed to have sighted was Antinous's deified spirit.
    l. 7, *stillenden*: *stillen* is "to soothe or placate," but also "to suckle a child." An-
tinous seems to enter a realm of consoling maternal earth deities—as if pass-
ing through a chthonic middle realm—on his way in Hadrian's imagination
from death by drowning (and the continued presence of grief) to stellar dei-
fication (and the finality of loss).

Der Tod der Geliebten

Er wußte nur vom Tod was alle wissen:
daß er uns nimmt und in das Stumme stößt.
Als aber sie, nicht von ihm fortgerissen,
nein, leis aus seinen Augen ausgelöst,

hinüberglitt zu unbekannten Schatten,
und als er fühlte, daß sie drüben nun
wie einen Mond ihr Mädchenlächeln hatten
und ihre Weise wohlzutun:

da wurden ihm die Toten so bekannt,
als wäre er durch sie mit einem jeden
ganz nah verwandt; er ließ die andern reden

und glaubte nicht und nannte jenes Land
das gutgelegene, das immersüße—
Und tastete es ab für ihre Füße.

The Death of the Beloved

He only knew of death what all men know:
that it takes and thrusts us into the silent.
But when she, not torn away from him,
no, gently loosened from his eyes,

drifted over toward unfamiliar shadows,
and when he felt that over there they now
like a moon had her youthful smile
and the kindness of her way:

then the dead grew so familiar to him,
as if he were through her to each one
closely tied: he let the others talk

and refused to listen and named that land
the goodly placed, the ever fragrant—
And felt out all its regions for her feet.

Klage um Jonathan

Ach sind auch Könige nicht von Bestand
und dürfen hingehn wie gemeine Dinge,
obwohl ihr Druck wie der der Siegelringe
sich widerbildet in das weiche Land.

Wie aber konntest du, so angefangen
mit deines Herzens Initial,
aufhören plötzlich: Wärme meiner Wangen.
O daß dich einer noch einmal
erzeugte, wenn sein Samen in ihm glänzt.

Irgend ein Fremder sollte dich zerstören,
und der dir innig war, ist nichts dabei
und muß sich halten und die Botschaft hören;
wie wunde Tiere auf den Lagern löhren,
möcht ich mich legen mit Geschrei:

denn da und da, an meinen scheusten Orten,
bist du mir ausgerissen wie das Haar,
das in den Achselhöhlen wächst und dorten,
wo ich ein Spiel für Frauen war,

bevor du meine dort verfitzten Sinne
aufsträhntest wie man einen Knaul entflicht;
da sah ich auf und wurde deiner inne:—
Jetzt aber gehst du mir aus dem Gesicht.

Lament for Jonathan

Ah that kings themselves last only for a time
and are allowed to pass like common objects,
though their weight, like that of a signet ring,
presses its image into the soft land.

But how could you, started the way you were
with your heart's initial letter,
all at once stop: warmth of my cheeks.
O that someone might once more
beget you, when his seed shines within him.

A random stranger was to destroy you,
and so your closest friend is nothing there
and must hold back and hear the message;
as wounded beasts roar out from under cover,
I'd like to ease myself with screaming:

for here and here, about my shyest places,
you are torn out of me like the hair
that grows within one's armpits, and there
where I was a sport for women

until you took the senses tangled there
and skeined them up as one unsnarls a clew;
I looked up then and you lodged deep inside me:—
But now you're disappearing from my sight.

II Samuel, i.

Tröstung des Elia

Er hatte das getan und dies, den Bund
wie jenen Altar wieder aufzubauen,
zu dem sein weitgeschleudertes Vertrauen
zurück als Feuer fiel von ferne, und
hatte er dann nicht Hunderte zerhauen,
weil sie ihm stanken mit dem Baal im Mund,
am Bache schlachtend bis ans Abendgrauen,

das mit dem Regengrau sich groß verband.
Doch als ihn von der Königin der Bote
nach solchem Werktag antrat und bedrohte,
da lief er wie ein Irrer in das Land,

so lange bis er unterm Ginsterstrauche
wie weggeworfen aufbrach in Geschrei
das in der Wüste brüllte: Gott, gebrauche
mich länger nicht. Ich bin entzwei.

Doch grade da kam ihn der Engel ätzen
mit einer Speise, die er tief empfing,
so daß er lange dann an Weideplätzen
und Wassern immer zum Gebirge ging,

zu dem der Herr um seinetwillen kam:
Im Sturme nicht und nicht im Sich-Zerspalten
der Erde, der entlang in schweren Falten
ein leeres Feuer ging, fast wie aus Scham
über des Ungeheuren ausgeruhtes
Hinstürzen zu dem angekommnen Alten,
der ihn im sanften Sausen seines Blutes
erschreckt und zugedeckt vernahm.

Comforting of Elijah

He had done everything to rebuild
the covenant (like that scattered altar)
to which his trust, flung out with such abandon,
fell back from far away like fire, and
had he not then crushed hundreds because
they stank to him with Baal inside their mouths,
slaughtering by the brook up to the evening,

whose gray dread banded with the rain's gray pall.
But when the queen's messenger approached
and—after such a day's work—threatened him,
he ran like a madman into the land

until at last among the desert bushes
as though thrown away he broke out in cries
that bellowed in the wilderness: God,
use me no longer. I am in pieces.

But just then the angel came to feed him,
with a meal that he took in so deeply
that for days he journeyed on past stream
and meadow, always toward that mountain

to which the Lord came only for his sake:
Not in the storm and not in the splitting-open
of the earth, along which in heavy folds
an empty fire went, almost as if from shame
at how the Inconceivable rushed forth
well-rested toward that just-arrived old man,
who in the soft pounding of his blood
frightened and cloak-enshrouded heard him.

I Kings, xviii–xix.

Saul unter den Propheten

Meinst du denn, daß man sich sinken sieht?
Nein, der König schien sich noch erhaben,
da er seinen starken Harfenknaben
töten wollte bis ins zehnte Glied.

Erst da ihn der Geist auf solchen Wegen
überfiel und auseinanderriß,
sah er sich im Innern ohne Segen,
und sein Blut ging in der Finsternis
abergläubig dem Gericht entgegen.

Wenn sein Mund jetzt troff und prophezeite,
war es nur, damit der Flüchtling weit
flüchten könne. So war dieses zweite
Mal. Doch einst: er hatte prophezeit

fast als Kind, als ob ihm jede Ader
mündete in einen Mund aus Erz;
Alle schritten, doch er schritt gerader.
Alle schrieen, doch ihm schrie das Herz.

Und nun war er nichts als dieser Haufen
umgestürzter Würden, Last auf Last;
und sein Mund war wie der Mund der Traufen,
der die Güsse, die zusammenlaufen,
fallen läßt, eh er sie faßt.

Saul among the Prophets

Does a man, then, observe his own decline?
No, the King felt himself still exalted
when he longed to kill his strong harp-boy
even unto the tenth generation.

Only when along such paths the Spirit
rushed down on him and ripped him apart,
did he see how void he was of blessing,
and his blood went in the gloom and darkness
up toward judgment, superstitiously.

If his mouth now dripped and prophesied,
it was just to let that fugitive
flee far away. Thus it was this second time.
Yet once before: he had prophesied

almost like a child, as if each vein
flowed straight into a mouth of bronze;
All strode, but he strode more erect.
All screamed, but it was his heart that screamed.

And now he was nothing but this heap
of overturned dignities, load upon load;
and his mouth was like the mouth of rain-gutters,
which lets the pourings, which run together,
fall out, before it's caught them.

I Samuel, xix, 8–24, x, 1–10.

Samuels Erscheinung vor Saul

Da schrie die Frau zu Endor auf: Ich sehe—
Der König packte sie am Arme: Wen?
Und da die Starrende beschrieb, noch ehe,
da war ihm schon, er hätte selbst gesehn:

Den, dessen Stimme ihn noch einmal traf:
Was störst du mich? Ich habe Schlaf.
Willst du, weil dir die Himmel fluchen
und weil der Herr sich vor dir schloß und schwieg,
in meinem Mund nach einem Siege suchen?
Soll ich dir meine Zähne einzeln sagen?
Ich habe nichts als sie . . . Es schwand. Da schrie
das Weib, die Hände vors Gesicht geschlagen,
als ob sie's sehen müßte: Unterlieg—

Und er, der in der Zeit, die ihm gelang,
das Volk wie ein Feldzeichen überragte,
fiel hin, bevor er noch zu klagen wagte:
so sicher war sein Untergang.

Die aber, die ihn wider Willen schlug,
hoffte, daß er sich faßte und vergäße;
und als sie hörte, daß er nie mehr äße,
ging sie hinaus und schlachtete und buk

und brachte ihn dazu, daß er sich setzte;
er saß wie einer, der zu viel vergißt:
alles was war, bis auf das Eine, Letzte.
Dann aß er wie ein Knecht zu Abend ißt.

Samuel's Appearance to Saul

With that the wife of Endor screamed: I see—
The King grabbed her by the arm: See whom?
And when—no, before—that staring one described,
it felt as if his own eyes had been seeing:

Him, whose voice once more struck home:
Why do you vex me? I am asleep.
Will you, because the heavens curse you
and because the Lord is closed to your approach,
seek in my mouth for a victory?
Shall I tell you one by one my teeth?
They're all I have . . . It vanished. With that
the woman screamed, hands flung before her face,
as if she'd been forced to see it: Give in—

And he, who in the days of his successes
had towered above his people like a battle-flag,
collapsed before he even dared lament:
so certain was his downfall.

But she, who had struck him against her will,
hoped he'd get hold of himself and forget;
and when she heard that he had stopped eating,
she went out and slaughtered and baked

and then persuaded him to take a seat;
he sat like someone who forgets too much:
all that ever was, up to the one, last thing.
Then he ate, like a worn-out farmhand eats.

I Samuel, xxviii.

Ein Prophet

Ausgedehnt von riesigen Gesichten,
hell vom Feuerschein aus dem Verlauf
der Gerichte, die ihn nie vernichten,—
sind die Augen, schauend unter dichten
Brauen. Und in seinem Innern richten
sich schon wieder Worte auf,

nicht die seinen (denn was wären seine
und wie schonend wären sie vertan)
andre, harte: Eisenstücke, Steine,
die er schmelzen muß wie ein Vulkan,

um sie in dem Ausbruch seines Mundes
auszuwerfen, welcher flucht und flucht;
während seine Stirne, wie des Hundes
Stirne, *das* zu tragen sucht,

was der Herr von seiner Stirne nimmt:
Dieser, Dieser, den sie alle fänden,
folgten sie den großen Zeigehänden,
die Ihn weisen wie Er ist: ergrimmt.

A Prophet

Stretched wide by gigantic visions,
bright from the fire's glare from that course
of judgments, which never destroy him,—
are his eyes, gazing beneath thick
brows. And already in his inmost self
words are building up again,

not his own (for what would his amount to
and how benignly they'd go to waste)
but other, hard ones: chunks of iron, stones,
which he must melt down like a volcano

in order to throw them out in the outbreak
of his mouth, which curses and curses;
while his forehead, like a dog's forehead,
tries to bear *that*

which the Lord from his own forehead takes:
This God, This God, whom they would all find,
if they'd follow the huge pointing hands
that reveal Him as He is: enraged.

Jeremia

Einmal war ich weich wie früher Weizen,
doch, du Rasender, du hast vermocht,
mir das hingehaltne Herz zu reizen,
daß es jetzt wie eines Löwen kocht.

Welchen Mund hast du mir zugemutet,
damals, da ich fast ein Knabe war:
eine Wunde wurde er: nun blutet
aus ihm Unglücksjahr um Unglücksjahr.

Täglich tönte ich von neuen Nöten,
die du, Unersättlicher, ersannst,
und sie konnten mir den Mund nicht töten;
sieh du zu, wie du ihn stillen kannst,

wenn, die wir zerstoßen und zerstören,
erst verloren sind und fernverlaufen
und vergangen sind in der Gefahr:
denn dann will ich in den Trümmerhaufen
endlich meine Stimme wiederhören,
die von Anfang an ein Heulen war.

Jeremiah

Once I was as tender as young wheat,
yet, you raging one, you have been able
to inflame the heart held out to you
so that now it boils like a lion's.

What a mouth you have demanded of me,
almost from the time I was a boy:
it became a wound: now year after
doom-laden year bleeds from it.

Each day I sounded with new afflictions,
which you, insatiate one, devised,
and they could not kill my mouth;
look to see how you can quiet it,

when those we devastate and crush
are finally lost and driven far away
and are perished in the danger:
for then I want in the heaps of rubble
at last to hear my voice again,
which was a howling from the very first.

Eine Sibylle

Einst, vor Zeiten, nannte man sie alt.
Doch sie blieb und kam dieselbe Straße
täglich. Und man änderte die Maße,
und man zählte sie wie einen Wald

nach Jahrhunderten. Sie aber stand
jeden Abend auf derselben Stelle,
schwarz wie eine alte Citadelle
hoch und hohl und ausgebrannt;

von den Worten, die sich unbewacht
wider ihren Willen in ihr mehrten,
immerfort umschrieen und umflogen,
während die schon wieder heimgekehrten
dunkel unter ihren Augenbogen
saßen, fertig für die Nacht.

A Sybil

Once, ages ago, they called her old.
But she lived on, and came down the same street
every day. And they changed the scale,
and like a forest told her age

by centuries. But she stood
every evening on the same place,
black like an ancient citadel,
tall and hollow and burnt out;

as the words, which left unchecked
would multiply in her against her will,
screamed and flew around her in incessant circles,
while those that had returned home
sat darkly beneath her eyebrows' arches,
waiting calmly for the night.

Absaloms Abfall

Sie hoben sie mit Geblitz:
der Sturm aus den Hörnern schwellte
seidene, breitgewellte
Fahnen. Der herrlich Erhellte
nahm im hochoffenen Zelte,
das jauchzendes Volk umstellte,
zehn Frauen in Besitz,

die (gewohnt an des alternden Fürsten
sparsame Nacht und Tat)
unter seinem Dürsten
wogten wie Sommersaat.

Dann trat er heraus zum Rate,
wie vermindert um nichts,
und jeder, der ihm nahte,
erblindete seines Lichts.

So zog er auch den Heeren
voran wie ein Stern dem Jahr;
über allen Speeren
wehte sein warmes Haar,
das der Helm nicht faßte,
und das er manchmal haßte,
weil es schwerer war
als seine reichsten Kleider.

Absalom's Rebellion

Lightning flashed as they raised them:
the storm from the horns swelled
silken, broadly billowing
flags. In the open rooftop tent,
surrounded by his rejoicing
throng, the magnificent enchanter
took ten women for his own,

while they (used to the aging king's
frugal night and deed)
swayed like summer crops
beneath his thirst.

Then he strode out toward the council
as if diminished not at all,
and everyone who came near him
was blinded by his light.

Thus too he led the troops,
like a star bringing in the year:
over all the lances waved
his warm, shining hair,
which escaped his helmet,
and which he sometimes hated,
since it weighed him down
more than his richest clothes.

Der König hatte geboten
daß man den Schönen schone.
Doch man sah ihn ohne
Helm an den bedrohten
Orten die ärgsten Knoten
zu roten Stücken von Toten
auseinanderhaun.
Dann wußte lange keiner
von ihm, bis plötzlich einer
schrie: Er hängt dort hinten
an den Terebinthen
mit hochgezogenen Braun.

Das war genug des Winks.
Joab, wie ein Jäger,
erspähte das Haar—: ein schräger
gedrehter Ast: da hings.
Er durchrannte den schlanken Kläger,
und seine Waffenträger
durchbohrten ihn rechts und links.

The king had commanded them
to deal gently with the prince.
But they saw him without
his helmet at the endangered
places hacking the most
desperate concentrations
into red bits of dead.
Then for a long time no one
knew of him, until suddenly
someone cried: He's hanging
back there on the big oak tree
with his brows stretched high.

That hint was all it took.
Joab, like a hunter,
searched out the hair—: a slanting
twisted branch: there it hung.
He ran through the slender plaintiff,
and his armorbearers
drilled through him left and right.

II Samuel, xiv–xviii.

Esther

Die Dienerinnen kämmten sieben Tage
die Asche ihres Grams und ihrer Plage
Neige und Niederschlag aus ihrem Haar,
und trugen es und sonnten es im Freien
und speisten es mit reinen Spezereien
noch diesen Tag und den: dann aber war

die Zeit gekommen, da sie, ungeboten,
zu keiner Frist, wie eine von den Toten
den drohend offenen Palast betrat,
um gleich, gelegt auf ihre Kammerfrauen,
am Ende ihres Weges *Den* zu schauen,
an dem man stirbt, wenn man ihm naht.

Er glänzte so, daß sie die Kronrubine
aufflammen fühlte, die sie an sich trug;
sie füllte sich ganz rasch mit seiner Miene
wie ein Gefäß und war schon voll genug

und floß schon über von des Königs Macht,
bevor sie noch den dritten Saal durchschritt,
der sie mit seiner Wände Malachit
grün überlief. Sie hatte nicht gedacht,

so langen Gang zu tun mit allen Steinen,
die schwerer wurden von des Königs Scheinen
und kalt von ihrer Angst. Sie ging und ging—

Und als sie endlich, fast von nahe, ihn,
aufruhend auf dem Thron von Turmalin,
sich türmen sah, so wirklich wie ein Ding:

Esther

Her servants combed for seven days
the ashes of her sorrow and the dregs
of sedimented anguish from her hair,
and carried it and sunned it in the open
and fed it with the purest spices
for two days more: but then that time

had come when she, uninvited, toward
no appointment, like someone from the dead
stepped through the gaping palace doors
to instantly, propped upon her women,
see stationed at her path's conclusion *Him*,
whom one approaches on pain of death.

He shone so, that she felt the royal rubies
which she bore upon herself flare up;
she filled up swiftly with his presence
like a vessel and was completely full

and overflowing from the king's power
before she'd walked the length of that third hall
which with its endless walls of malachite
spilled greenly over her. She hadn't thought

to make so long a walk with all those stones,
which grew heavier from the king's shining
and cold from her fear. She walked on and on—

And when at last, almost within reach, she saw him,
as he reposed on his throne of tourmaline,
tower up, as real as a thing:

empfing die rechte von den Dienerinnen
die Schwindende und hielt sie zu dem Sitze.
Er rührte sie mit seines Szepters Spitze:
... und sie begriff es ohne Sinne, innen.

the woman on her right could feel her
growing dizzy and held her toward the seat.
He touched her with his scepter's tip:
. . . and through her swoon it reached her, deep within.

Esther, iv and v, and Apocrypha.

Der Aussätzige König

Da trat auf seiner Stirn der Aussatz aus
und stand auf einmal unter seiner Krone
als wär er König über allen Graus,
der in die Andern fuhr, die fassungsohne

hinstarrten nach dem furchtbaren Vollzug
an jenem, welcher, schmal wie ein Verschnürter,
erwartete, daß einer nach ihm schlug;
doch noch war keiner Manns genug:
als machte ihn nur immer unberührter
die neue Würde, die sich übertrug.

The Leper King

Then on his brow the leprosy broke out
and stood there suddenly beneath his crown
as though it were king of all the horror
that passed into the others, who dumbstruck

stared at that awful consummation
making him who, pulled in like a mummy,
expected someone to lash out at him;
but still no one was man enough:
as if he'd only grown more untouchable
through that new dignity, which was contagious.

The Leper King: Not Charles VI of France, the Leper King of Rilke's *Malte Laurids Brigge*, but King Uzziah of II Chronicles 16–21, stricken in the temple as the priests whose prerogatives he had usurped look on in amazement.

Legende von den drei Lebendigen und den drei Toten

Drei Herren hatten mit Falken gebeizt
und freuten sich auf das Gelag.
Da nahm sie der Greis in Beschlag
und führte. Die Reiter hielten gespreizt
vor dem dreifachen Sarkophag,

der ihnen dreimal entgegenstank,
in den Mund, in die Nase, ins Sehn;
und sie wußten es gleich: da lagen lang
drei Tote mitten im Untergang
und ließen sich gräßlich gehn.

Und sie hatten nur noch ihr Jägergehör
reinlich hinter dem Sturmbandlör;
doch da zischte der Alte sein:
—Sie gingen nicht durch das Nadelöhr
und gehen niemals—hinein.

Nun blieb ihnen noch ihr klares Getast,
das stark war vom Jagen und heiß;
doch das hatte ein Frost von hinten gefaßt
und trieb ihm Eis in den Schweiß.

Legend of the Three Living
and the Three Dead

Three lords had hawked with falcons
and looked forward to the feast.
Then the old man seized their fancies
and led them on. The riders pulled in hard
before the threefold sarcophagus

whose stench three times pressed toward them,
into their mouths, into their noses, into their eyes;
and they knew at once: three dead lay there
long held in the midst of declining
and horribly let themselves go.

And they only had left their sharp hunter's ear
still clean behind their chin-straps;
but then the old man hissed his:
—They didn't go through the needle's eye
and never will—into that.

Now just their clear sense of touch remained,
which was strong from hunting and hot;
but a frost had seized that from behind
and was making its sweat ooze ice.

Der König von Münster

Der König war geschoren;
nun ging ihm die Krone zu weit
und bog ein wenig die Ohren,
in die von Zeit zu Zeit

gehässiges Gelärme
aus Hungermäulern fand.
Er saß, von wegen der Wärme,
auf seiner rechten Hand,

mürrisch und schwergesäßig.
Er fühlte sich nicht mehr echt:
der Herr in ihm war mäßig,
und der Beischlaf war schlecht.

The King of Münster

His Highness had been fleeced;
the crown now was too big to fit
and bent down a bit his ears,
through which from time to time

a rancorous commotion
from famished mouths made way.
He sat (to try to warm it)
on his right hand,

morose and heavy-bottomed.
He no longer felt exalted;
the Lord in him was paltry,
and he'd gone bad in bed.

The King of Münster: John of Leyden, a former Münster tailor who became
leader of that city's Anabaptist uprisings of 1534–35. He was executed in
1536.

Toten-Tanz

Sie brauchen kein Tanz-Orchester;
sie hören in sich ein Geheule
als wären sie Eulennester.
Ihr Ängsten näßt wie eine Beule,
und der Vorgeruch ihrer Fäule
ist noch ihr bester Geruch.

Sie fassen den Tänzer fester,
den rippenbetreßten Tänzer,
den Galan, den ächten Ergänzer
zu einem ganzen Paar.
Und er lockert der Ordensschwester
über dem Haar das Tuch;
sie tanzen ja unter Gleichen.
Und er zieht der wachslichtbleichen
leise die Lesezeichen
aus ihrem Stunden-Buch.

Bald wird ihnen allen zu heiß,
sie sind zu reich gekleidet;
beißender Schweiß verleidet
ihnen Stirne und Steiß
und Schauben und Hauben und Steine;
sie wünschen, sie wären nackt
wie ein Kind, ein Verrückter und Eine:
die tanzen noch immer im Takt.

Dance of Death

They need no dance band;
they hear in themselves a howling
as if they were owls' nests.
Their dread oozes like a boil,
and the strong intimation of their rot
is the best of what they smell.

They clasped the dancer more tightly,
the rib-braided dancer,
the gallant, the true completer
to a perfect pair.
And he loosens for the nursing-sister
the cloth above her hair:
they dance, after all, among equals.
And softly for that night-light pale one
he draws the passage-markers
from her book of hours.

Soon they all grow too hot,
they are too richly clothed;
biting sweat makes them
hate brow and rump
and cloak and cap and stone;
they wish they were naked
like a child, a madman, and a whore:
those still dance to the tune.

Das jüngste Gericht

So erschrocken, wie sie nie erschraken,
ohne Ordnung, oft durchlocht und locker,
hocken sie in dem geborstnen Ocker
ihres Ackers, nicht von ihren Laken

abzubringen, die sie liebgewannen.
Aber Engel kommen an, um Öle
einzuträufeln in die trocknen Pfannen
und um jedem in die Achselhöhle

das zu legen, was er in dem Lärme
damals seines Lebens nicht entweihte;
denn dort hat es noch ein wenig Wärme,

daß es nicht des Herren Hand erkälte
oben, wenn er es aus jeder Seite
leise greift, zu fühlen, ob es gälte.

The Last Judgment

So frightened, beyond their wildest fright,
disordered, often full of holes and loose,
they hunker down in the exploded furrows
of their field, not to be dissuaded

of their shrouds, which they have grown to like.
But angels come, and begin at once
to trickle oil into the dried-out sockets
and to put in each one's armpits

whatever in the tumult of that life
its user managed not to desecrate;
for it still has a bit of warmth there,

so that it won't chill the hand of God
when, up above, from either side he gently
grasps it, to feel if it's still good.

Die Versuchung

Nein, es half nicht, daß er sich die scharfen
Stacheln einhieb in das geile Fleisch;
alle seine trächtigen Sinne warfen
unter kreißendem Gekreisch

Frühgeburten: schiefe, hingeschielte
kriechende und fliegende Gesichte,
Nichte, deren nur auf ihn erpichte
Bosheit sich verband und mit ihm spielte.

Und schon hatten seine Sinne Enkel;
denn das Pack war fruchtbar in der Nacht
und in immer bunterem Gesprenkel
hingehudelt und verhundertfacht.
Aus dem Ganzen ward ein Trank gemacht:
seine Hände griffen lauter Henkel,
und der Schatten schob sich auf wie Schenkel
warm und zu Umarmungen erwacht—.

Und da schrie er nach dem Engel, schrie:
Und der Engel kam in seinem Schein
und war da: und jagte sie
wieder in den Heiligen hinein,

daß er mit Geteufel und Getier
in sich weiterringe wie seit Jahren
und sich Gott, den lange noch nicht klaren,
innen aus dem Jäsen destillier.

The Temptation

No, it didn't help, that he drove sharp
thorns into his lecherous flesh;
all his pregnant senses threw forth
amid shrill laboring shrieking

half-cocked births: lopsided, leeringly envisaged
crawling and flying apparitions,
nothings, whose malice, bent on him alone,
united and had fun with him.

And already his senses had grandchildren:
for the pack was fruitful in the night
and in wilder and wilder specklings
botched itself and multiplied by hundreds.
From the whole mix a drink was made:
his hands grasped sheer handles,
and the shadows slid open like thighs
warm and wakened for embracing—.

And then he screamed for the angel, screamed:
And the angel came in his halo
and was present: and drove them
back inside the saint again,

that he might wrestle on within himself
with beasts and demons as for years now
and make God, the as yet far from clear,
out of the ferment inwardly distill.

Der Alchimist

Seltsam verlächelnd schob der Laborant
den Kolben fort, der halbberuhigt rauchte.
Er wußte jetzt, was er noch brauchte,
damit der sehr erlauchte Gegenstand

da drin entstände. Zeiten brauchte er,
Jahrtausende für sich und diese Birne
in der es brodelte; im Hirn Gestirne
und im Bewußtsein mindestens das Meer.

Das Ungeheuere, das er gewollt,
er ließ es los in dieser Nacht. Es kehrte
zurück zu Gott und in sein altes Maß;

er aber, lallend wie ein Trunkenbold,
lag über dem Geheimfach und begehrte
den Brocken Gold, den er besaß.

The Alchemist

With a twisted smile the lab assistant
shoved the flask away that smoked half-calmed.
He knew at last what he still needed
to make the venerable thing

spring up inside it. He needed ages,
millennia for himself and this glass pear
in which it bubbled; needed stars in his brain
and in his consciousness at least the sea.

The enormity his will had seized on
he let go that same night. It went
back to God and to its ancient measure;

but he, babbling like a drunkard,
lay across the secret drawer and craved
the chunk of gold that he possessed.

Der Reliquienschrein

Draussen wartete auf alle Ringe
und auf jedes Kettenglied
Schicksal, das nicht ohne sie geschieht.
Drinnen waren sie nur Dinge, Dinge
die er schmiedete; denn vor dem Schmied
war sogar die Krone, die er bog,
nur ein Ding, ein zitterndes und eines
das er finster wie im Zorn erzog
zu dem Tragen eines reinen Steines.

Seine Augen wurden immer kälter
von dem kalten täglichen Getränk;
aber als der herrliche Behälter
(goldgetrieben, köstlich, vielkarätig)
fertig vor ihm stand, das Weihgeschenk,
daß darin ein kleines Handgelenk
fürder wohne, weiß und wundertätig:

blieb er ohne Ende auf den Knien,
hingeworfen, weinend, nichtmehr wagend,
seine Seele niederschlagend
vor dem ruhigen Rubin,
der ihn zu gewahren schien
und ihn, plötzlich um sein Dasein fragend,
ansah wie aus Dynastien.

The Reliquary

Outside Fate waited on all the rings
and on each new chain-link,
since without them it only looms.
Inside they remained things, things
that he forged; for before the smith
even the crown (which he bent)
was just a thing, a trembling thing
that he brought up sternly, as if in anger,
for the bearing of a flawless stone.

His eyes kept growing colder
from the cold drink that each day gave;
but when the glorious container
(gold-embossed, exquisite, many-carated)
stood before him finished, the votive gift,
inside of which a small wrist might
one day dwell, white and working miracles:

he stayed an eternity on his knees,
cast down, weeping, no longer daring,
lowering his soul
before the restful ruby,
which seemed to grow aware of him
and, suddenly asking him his purpose,
gazed on him as if from dynasties.

Das Gold

Denk es wäre nicht: es hätte müssen
endlich in den Bergen sich gebären
und sich niederschlagen in den Flüssen
aus dem Wollen, aus dem Gären

ihres Willens; aus der Zwang-Idee,
daß ein Erz ist über allen Erzen.
Weithin warfen sie aus ihren Herzen
immer wieder Meroë

an den Rand der Lande, in den Äther,
über das Erfahrene hinaus;
und die Söhne brachten manchmal später
das Verheißene der Väter,
abgehärtet und verhehrt, nachhaus;

wo es anwuchs eine Zeit, um dann
fortzugehn von den an ihm Geschwächten,
die es niemals liebgewann.
Nur (so sagt man) in den letzten Nächten
steht es auf und sieht sie an.

Gold

Imagine that it weren't: it would have had
at last to birth itself inside the mountains
and sediment itself inside the rivers
from the urging, from the ferment

of their wills; from the driving notion
that an ore exists beyond all ores.
Far off they cast out of their hearts
again and again Meroë

out to the land's edge, into the ether,
beyond the regions of the known;
and the sons brought sometime later
that promised to the fathers,
hardened and stripped of dignity, home;

where it grew for a time, and then
went away from those who'd weakened from it,
those it never came to like.
Only (so it's said) in the last nights
does it rise up and gaze on them.

l. 8, *Meroë*: the ruined capital of Ethiopia, fabled as the richest gold-producing region of the ancient world.

Der Stylit

Völker schlugen über ihm zusammen,
die er küren durfte und verdammen;
und erratend, daß er sich verlor,
klomm er aus dem Volksgeruch mit klammen
Händen einen Säulenschaft empor,

der noch immer stieg und nichts mehr hob,
und begann, allein auf seiner Fläche,
ganz von vorne seine eigne Schwäche
zu vergleichen mit des Herren Lob;

und da war kein Ende: er verglich;
und der Andre wurde immer größer.
Und die Hirten, Ackerbauer, Flößer
sahn ihn klein und außer sich

immer mit dem ganzen Himmel reden,
eingeregnet manchmal, manchmal licht;
und sein Heulen stürzte sich auf jeden,
so als heulte er ihm ins Gesicht.
Doch er sah seit Jahren nicht,

wie der Menge Drängen und Verlauf
unten unaufhörlich sich ergänzte,
und das Blanke an den Fürsten glänzte
lange nicht so hoch hinauf.

The Stylite

From all sides he was beseiged by nations
which he might deem elected and condemn;
and grasping finally that he lost himself,
he climbed out of the collective stench
with clammy hands along a column's shaft

that still rose up yet lifted nothing,
and began, alone upon its surface,
to weigh once more from the beginning
his own weakness against the Lord's praise;

and there was no end to it: he compared;
and the Other kept growing greater.
And shepherds, raftsmen, farmers at their plow
saw him small and almost crazed

forever talking with the boundless sky,
dimmed by rainstorms sometimes, sometimes bright;
and his howling plunged down upon them all
as if he howled into each one's face.
Yet he hadn't seen for years

how the press and issue of the crowd
below constantly renewed itself,
and the polish on the princes long since
had ceased to shine so high.

Aber wenn er oben, fast verdammt
und von ihrem Widerstand zerschunden,
einsam mit verzweifeltem Geschreie
schüttelte die täglichen Dämonen:
fielen langsam auf die erste Reihe
schwer und ungeschickt aus seinen Wunden
große Würmer in die offnen Kronen
und vermehrten sich im Samt.

But when he above, almost condemned
and from their resistance flayed to pieces,
alone there with despair-filled cries
tried to shake the daily demons:
huge worms fell slowly from his wounds
with heavy awkward writhing
into the first row's open crowns
and multiplied in velvet.

Stylite: Christian ascetic who lived standing on top of a column (Greek *stylos*).
The poem probably refers to the life of the first stylite, Saint Simeon (c. 390–
459), who, after being expelled from a monastery for his overly severe mor-
tifications, became a hermit at the foot of Mount Teleanissae, moving after
three years to its top, where he began to attract huge crowds. To escape them
he erected, in 423, a ten-foot pillar, and spent the rest of his life on successively
higher ones. His last pillar measured sixty feet.

Die Ägyptische Maria

Seit sie damals, bettheiß, als die Hure
übern Jordan floh und, wie ein Grab
gebend, stark und unvermischt das pure
Herz der Ewigkeit zu trinken gab,

wuchs ihr frühes Hingegebensein
unaufhaltsam an zu solcher Größe,
daß sie endlich, wie die ewige Blöße
Aller, aus vergilbtem Elfenbein

dalag in der dürren Haare Schelfe.
Und ein Löwe kreiste; und ein Alter
rief ihn winkend an, daß er ihm helfe:

(und so gruben sie zu zwein.)

Und der Alte neigte sie hinein.
Und der Löwe, wie ein Wappenhalter,
saß dabei und hielt den Stein.

The Egyptian Mary

From the time that she fled, bed-hot,
across Jordan as the whore, and, yielding
like a grave, gave up her pure heart,
strong and unmixed, to Eternity to drink,

her early self-surrendering grew
unchecked to such a greatness that at last,
like the eternal nakedness of all,
made from yellowed ivory

she lay there in her dry hair's husk.
And a lion circled; and an old man
called to him, and beckoned him to help:

(and so the two together dug).

And the old man lowered her inside.
And the lion, like a shield-supporter,
sat at the edge and held the stone.

St. Mary of Egypt, whose story is told in the *Golden Legend*.

Kreuzigung

Längst geübt, zum kahlen Galgenplatze
irgend ein Gesindel hinzudrängen,
ließen sich die schweren Knechte hängen,
dann und wann nur eine große Fratze

kehrend nach den abgetanen Drein.
Aber oben war das schlechte Henkern
rasch getan; und nach dem Fertigsein
ließen sich die freien Männer schlenkern.

Bis der eine (fleckig wie ein Selcher)
sagte: Hauptmann, dieser hat geschrien.
Und der Hauptmann sah vom Pferde: Welcher?
und es war ihm selbst, er hätte ihn

den Elia rufen hören. Alle
waren zuzuschauen voller Lust,
und sie hielten, daß er nicht verfalle,
gierig ihm die ganze Essiggalle
an sein schwindendes Gehust.

Denn sie hofften noch ein ganzes Spiel
und vielleicht den kommenden Elia.
Aber hinten ferne schrie Maria,
und er selber brüllte und verfiel.

Crucifixion

Long practiced as they were in pushing
some riffraff to the barren gallows-place,
the heavy henchmen hung loosely about,
turning now and then just a large grimace

toward the disposed-of, done-away-with three.
But up there the wretched hanging-job
was swiftly done; and in the aftermath
the free men dangled aimlessly about.

Until the one (spattered like a butcher)
said: Captain, this one just cried out.
And the captain looked from his horse:
Which one? and it seemed to him too

that he had heard him call Elijah.
They all were avid to be lookers-on,
and greedily, to keep him from collapsing,
held out the entire vinegar-gall
to his fast-dwindling cough.

For they hoped the play was still in progress
and that perhaps Elijah was to come.
But far back in the distance Mary screamed,
and he himself bellowed and caved in.

Der Auferstandene

Er vermochte niemals bis zuletzt
ihr zu weigern oder abzuneinen,
daß sie ihrer Liebe sich berühme;
und sie sank ans Kreuz in dem Kostüme
eines Schmerzes, welches ganz besetzt
war mit ihrer Liebe größten Steinen.

Aber da sie dann, um ihn zu salben,
an das Grab kam, Tränen im Gesicht,
war er auferstanden ihrethalben,
daß er seliger ihr sage: Nicht—

Sie begriff es erst in ihrer Höhle,
wie er ihr, gestärkt durch seinen Tod,
endlich das Erleichternde der Öle
und des Rührens Vorgefühl verbot,

um aus ihr die Liebende zu formen
die sich nicht mehr zum Geliebten neigt,
weil sie, hingerissen von enormen
Stürmen, seine Stimme übersteigt.

The Arisen

He was never able, right up to the end,
to refuse her or break by saying "no"
her way of feeling famous in her love;
and she sank at the cross in the costume
of a grief that was completely studded
with her love's most ostentatious stones.

But when she then, meaning to anoint him,
arrived at the tomb, with tears in her face,
he had risen just for her sake, that he
might say to her with deeper bliss: Don't—

She only understood it in her cave—
how he, grown stronger through his death,
at last forbade her the oil's assuaging
and the presentiment of touch,

in order to make from her the lover
who is drawn no longer toward the loved,
since she, transported by enormous
storms, ascends beyond his voice's reach.

Magnificat

Sie kam den Hang herauf, schon schwer, fast ohne
an Trost zu glauben, Hoffnung oder Rat;
doch da die hohe tragende Matrone
ihr ernst und stolz entgegentrat

und alles wußte ohne ihr Vertrauen,
da war sie plötzlich an ihr ausgeruht;
vorsichtig hielten sich die vollen Frauen,
bis daß die junge sprach: Mir is zumut,

als wär ich, Liebe, von nun an für immer.
Gott schüttet in der Reichen Eitelkeit
fast ohne hinzusehen ihren Schimmer;
doch sorgsam sucht er sich ein Frauenzimmer
und füllt sie an mit seiner fernsten Zeit.

Daß er mich fand. Bedenk nur; und Befehle
um meinetwillen gab von Stern zu Stern—.

Verherrliche und hebe, meine Seele,
so hoch du kannst: den HERRN.

Magnificat

She came up the slope, heavy, almost unable
to believe in comfort, hope, or counsel;
but then when that stately pregnant matron
with pride and solemnity approached her

and knew everything without her confiding,
then beside her suddenly she was rested;
cautiously the full women held each other,
until the young one spoke: I feel as if

from now on, love, I am for ever.
God pours into the wealthy's vanity
almost without paying heed its glitter;
yet carefully seeks himself a woman
and fills her with his farthest time.

That he found *me*. Imagine; and issued
for my sake his commands from star to star—.

O glorify with all your might, my soul,
and raise on high: the LORD.

Adam

Staunend steht er an der Kathedrale
steilem Aufstieg, nah der Fensterrose,
wie erschreckt von der Apotheose,
welche wuchs und ihn mit einem Male

niederstellte über die und die.
Und er ragt und freut sich seiner Dauer
schlicht entschlossen; als der Ackerbauer
der begann, und der nicht wußte, wie

aus dem fertig-vollen Garten Eden
einen Ausweg in die neue Erde
finden. Gott war schwer zu überreden;

und er drohte ihm, statt zu gewähren,
immer wieder, daß er sterben werde.
Doch der Mensch bestand: sie wird gebären.

Adam

Amazed he stands at the cathedral's
steep ascent, close to the rose window,
as though startled by the apotheosis,
which grew and then all at once

placed him down over these below.
And he stands tall and exults in his duration,
simply determined; as the ground-tiller
who began, and who didn't know how

from the full-finished garden of Eden
to find a way out into the new earth.
God was hard to persuade;

and instead of granting, kept threatening,
over and over, that he would die.
But the man persisted: she will give birth.

Eva

Einfach steht sie an der Kathedrale
großem Aufstieg, nah der Fensterrose,
mit dem Apfel in der Apfelpose,
schuldlos-schuldig ein für alle Male

an dem Wachsenden, das sie gebar,
seit sie aus dem Kreis der Ewigkeiten
liebend fortging, um sich durchzustreiten
durch die Erde, wie ein junges Jahr.

Ach, sie hätte gern in jenem Land
noch ein wenig weilen mögen, achtend
auf der Tiere eintracht und Verstand.

Doch da sie den Mann entschlossen fand,
ging sie mit ihm, nach dem Tode trachtend;
und sie hatte Gott noch kaum gekannt.

Eve

Simply she stands at the cathedral's
great ascent, close to the rose window,
holding the apple in the apple-pose,
guiltless-guilty once and for all time

of the growing she gave birth to
when from the circle of the eternities
she lovingly went forth, to battle
her way through the earth like a young year.

Ah, she'd have gladly lingered in that land
for just a bit longer, attending
to the animals' insight and accord.

But since she found the man determined,
she went with him, aspiring after Death;
and she had hardly got to know God.

Irre im Garten

Dijon

Noch schließt die aufgegebene Kartause
sich um den Hof, als würde etwas heil.
Auch die sie jetzt bewohnen, haben Pause
und nehmen nicht am Leben draußen teil.

Was irgend kommen konnte, das verlief.
Nun gehn sie gerne mit bekannten Wegen,
und trennen sich und kommen sich entgegen,
als ob sie kreisten, willig, primitiv.

Zwar manche pflegen dort die Frühlingsbeete,
demütig, dürftig, hingekniet;
aber sie haben, wenn es keiner sieht,
eine verheimlichte, verdrehte

Gebärde für das zarte frühe Gras,
ein prüfendes, verschüchtertes Liebkosen:
denn das ist freundlich, und das Rot der Rosen
wird vielleicht drohend sein und Übermaß

und wird vielleicht schon wieder übersteigen,
was ihre Seele wiederkennt und weiß.
Dies aber läßt sich noch verschweigen:
wie gut das Gras ist und wie leis.

Lunatics in the Garden

Dijon

The abandoned monastery still closes
around the courtyard, as though a wound were healing.
Those who live there now also enjoy recess
and take no part in the life outside.

Whatever could happen came and went.
Now they walk gladly with familiar paths,
and separate and come upon each other
as though they circled, willing, primitive.

Some of them, true, tend the spring beds there,
humble, wretched, down on their knees;
but they have, when no one sees it,
a surreptitious, twisted

gesture for the tender early grass,
a testing, half-afraid caressing:
for that is friendly, and the roses' red
may grow menacing and too intense

and may once again take them beyond
what their souls recognize and know.
But this can still be kept a secret:
how good the grass is and how soft.

Die Irren

Und sie schweigen, weil die Scheidewände
weggenommen sind aus ihrem Sinn,
und die Stunden, da man sie verstände,
heben an und gehen hin.

Nächtens oft, wenn sie ans Fenster treten:
plötzlich ist es alles gut.
Ihre Hände liegen im Konkreten,
und das Herz is hoch und könnte beten,
und die Augen schauen ausgeruht

auf den unverhofften, oftentstellten
Garten im beruhigten Geviert,
der im Widerschein der fremden Welten
weiterwächst und niemals sich verliert.

The Lunatics

And they say nothing, since the dividing walls
inside their minds are taken down,
and the hours when one would understand them
come along and go away.

Often at night, when they step to the window:
suddenly it all feels right.
Their hands lie in what's concrete,
and their hearts are lifted and could pray,
and their eyes gaze rested

on the unexpected, oft-disfigured
garden inside the quieted-down square,
which in the reflections of the strange worlds
grows on and on and never gets lost.

Aus dem Leben eines Heiligen

Er kannte Ängste, deren Eingang schon
wie Sterben war und nicht zu überstehen.
Sein Herz erlernte, langsam durchzugehen;
er zog es groß wie einen Sohn.

Und namenlose Nöte kannte er,
finster und ohne Morgen wie Verschläge;
und seine Seele gab er folgsam her,
da sie erwachsen war, auf daß sie läge

bei ihrem Bräutigam und Herrn; und blieb
allein zurück an einem solchen Orte,
wo das Alleinsein alles übertrieb,
und wohnte weit und wollte niemals Worte.

Aber dafür, nach Zeit und Zeit, erfuhr
er auch das Glück, sich in die eignen Hände,
damit er eine Zärtlichkeit empfände,
zu legen wie die ganze Kreatur.

From the Life of a Saint

He came to know fears whose entrances
were like death and not to be endured.
His heart learned to go through slowly;
he brought it up like a son.

And he came to know nameless afflictions,
that were dark and morningless like dungeons;
and he gave up his soul obediently
when it was grown, so that it might lie

beside its lord and bridegroom; and stayed
behind alone in the sort of place
where aloneness exaggerates everything,
and dwelt far off and never wished for words.

But in recompense, after so much time
he also learned, that he might feel
a tenderness, the bliss of being held,
like all creation, in his own hands.

Die Bettler

Du wußtest nicht, was den Haufen
ausmacht. Ein Fremder fand
Bettler darin. Sie verkaufen
das Hohle aus ihrer Hand.

Sie zeigen dem Hergereisten
ihren Mund voll Mist,
und er darf (er kann es sich leisten)
sehn, wie ihr Aussatz frißt.

Es zergeht in ihren zerrührten
Augen sein fremdes Gesicht;
und sie freuen sich des Verführten
und speien, wenn er spricht.

The Beggars

You didn't know what the heap
was made of. A foreigner found
beggars in it. They sell
the hollows from their hands.

They show the one who's journeyed here
their mouths full of muck,
and he may (he can afford it)
see how their leprosy eats.

In their weirdly devastated
eyes his foreign face starts melting;
and they exult in his downfall
and spit when he speaks.

Fremde Familie

So wie der Staub, der irgenwie beginnt
und nirgends ist, zu unerklärtem Zwecke
an einem leeren Morgen in der Ecke
in die man sieht, ganz rasch zu Grau gerinnt,

so bildeten sie sich, wer weiß aus was,
im letzten Augenblick vor deinen Schritten
und waren etwas Ungewisses mitten
im nassen Niederschlag der Gasse, das

nach dir verlangte. Oder nicht nach dir.
Denn eine Stimme, wie vom vorigen Jahr,
sang dich zwar an und blieb doch ein Geweine;
und eine Hand, die wie geliehen war,
kam zwar hervor und nahm doch nicht die deine.
Wer kommt denn noch? Wen meinen diese vier?

Foreign Family

Just as the dust, which somehow begins
and is nowhere, will swiftly clot to gray—
for some unexplained reason on an empty
morning in the corner into which you look—

so they took shape, who knows from what,
in the last instant before your footsteps
and were an uncertain something amid
the damp detritus of the alley,

that longed for you. Or not for you.
For a voice, as from the year just past,
did sing to you, and yet remained a weeping;
and a hand, which was as if extended,
did reach out, and yet didn't take your own.
Who then still comes? Whom do these four mean?

Leichen-Wäsche

Sie hatten sich an ihn gewöhnt. Doch als
die Küchenlampe kam und unruhig brannte
im dunkeln Luftzug, war der Unbekannte
ganz unbekannt. Sie wuschen seinen Hals,

und da sie nichts von seinem Schicksal wußten,
so logen sie ein anderes zusamm,
fortwährend waschend. Eine mußte husten
und ließ solang den schweren Essigschwamm

auf dem Gesicht. Da gab es eine Pause
auch für die zweite. Aus der harten Bürste
klopften die Tropfen; während seine grause
gekrampfte Hand dem ganzen Hause
beweisen wollte, daß ihn nicht mehr dürste.

Und er bewies. Sie nahmen wie betreten
eiliger jetzt mit einem kurzen Huster
die Arbeit auf, so daß an den Tapeten
ihr krummer Schatten in dem stummen Muster

sich wand und wälzte wie in einem Netze,
bis daß die Waschenden zu Ende kamen.
Die Nacht im vorhanglosen Fensterrahmen
war rücksichtslos. Und einer ohne Namen
lag bar und reinlich da und gab Gesetze.

Corpse-Washing

They had grown used to him. But when
the kitchen lamp came and burned restlessly
in the dark draft, the one unknown there
was utterly unknown. They washed his neck,

and since they knew nothing of his fate,
they made up another one between them,
all the while washing. The first had to cough
and left the heavy vinegar-soaked sponge

lying on his face. Then there was a pause
while the other rested. From her hard brush
the drops kept falling; while his terrible
cramped hand tried to make the whole room see
that he no longer thirsted.

And he succeeded. With a short cough,
as if embarrassed, they took up the work
more urgently, so that on the wallpaper
their hunched shadows writhed and twisted

in the mute patterns as though in a net,
until the washings came to an end.
The night in the curtainless window-frame
was pitiless. And one without names
lay there bare and clean and issued laws.

Eine von den Alten

Paris

Abends manchmal (weißt du, wie das tut?)
wenn sie plötzlich stehn und rückwärts nicken
und ein Lächeln, wie aus lauter Flicken,
zeigen unter ihrem halben Hut.

Neben ihnen ist dann ein Gebäude,
endlos, und sie locken dich entlang
mit dem Rätsel ihrer Räude,
mit dem Hut, dem Umhang und dem Gang.

Mit der Hand, die hinten unterm Kragen
heimlich wartet und verlangt nach dir:
wie um deine Hände einzuschlagen
in ein aufgehobenes Papier.

One of the Old Women

Paris

In the evenings sometimes (you know how it feels?)
when they suddenly stop and nod backwards
and show you from under their half-hats
a smile that seems made of patches . . .

Next to them then is a building,
endless, and they lure you along
with the riddle of their scabs,
with the hat, the shawl, and the walk.

With the hand, which under the collar's nape
waits in secret and longs for you:
as if it wished to wrap your hands
in a scrap of picked-up paper.

Der Blinde

Paris

Sieh, er geht und unterbricht die Stadt,
die nicht ist auf seiner dunkeln Stelle,
wie ein dunkler Sprung durch eine helle
Tasse geht. Und wie auf einem Blatt

ist auf ihm der Widerschein der Dinge
aufgemalt; er nimmt ihn nicht hinein.
Nur sein Fühlen rührt sich, so als finge
es die Welt in kleinen Wellen ein:

eine Stille, einen Widerstand—,
und dann scheint er wartend wen zu wählen:
hingegeben hebt er seine Hand,
festlich fast, wie um sich zu vermählen.

The Blind Man

Paris

Look: he walks and interrupts the city,
which does not exist on his dark place,
the way a dark crack goes through a bright
cup. And as on an empty page

the reflections that things make are scrawled
on him; he doesn't take them in.
Only his feeling stirs, as if it caught
the world in small waves:

a stillness, a resistance—,
and then he seems waiting whom to choose:
totally absorbed he lifts his hand,
festively almost, as if for marriage.

Eine Welke

Leicht, wie nach ihrem Tode
trägt sie die Handschuh, das Tuch.
Ein Duft aus ihrer Kommode
verdrängte den lieben Geruch,

an dem sie sich früher erkannte.
Jetzt fragte sie lange nicht, wer
sie sei (: eine ferne Verwandte),
und geht in Gedanken umher

und sorgt für ein ängstliches Zimmer,
das sie ordnet und schont,
weil es vielleicht noch immer
dasselbe Mädchen bewohnt.

Faded

Lightly, as after her death,
she wears her gloves, her shawl.
A fragrance from her chest of drawers
has driven out the cherished smell

by which she used to know herself.
Now she has long ceased asking
who she is (: a distant relative),
and walks about lost in thought

and looks after a fastidious room,
which she arranges and protects,
since the same young girl
may even now be living there.

Abendmahl

Ewiges will zu uns. Wer hat die Wahl
und trennt die großen und geringen Kräfte?
Erkennst du durch das Dämmern der Geschäfte
im klaren Hinterraum das Abendmahl:

wie sie sichs halten und wie sie sichs reichen
und in der Handlung schlicht und schwer beruhn.
Aus ihren Händen heben sich die Zeichen;
sie wissen nicht, daß sie sie tun

und immer neu mit irgendwelchen Worten
einsetzen, was man trinkt und was man teilt.
Denn da ist keiner, der nicht allerorten
heimlich von hinnen geht, indem er weilt.

Und sitzt nicht immer einer unter ihnen,
der seine Eltern, die ihm ängstlich dienen,
wegschenkt an ihre abgetane Zeit?
(Sie zu verkaufen, ist ihm schon zu weit.)

Evening Meal

Things eternal want to join us. Who chooses,
and separates the great and lesser powers?
Can't you see through the twilight of the shops
the last supper shining in the back room:

how they hold it there and pass it on
and in those actions gravely, simply rest.
From their hands the signs are rising;
they don't know that they perform them,

and newly with each exchange of words
establish what one drinks and what one shares.
For there is no one anyplace who isn't
secretly departing, even as he stays.

And doesn't someone always sit among them
who gives away his parents, still anxiously
serving him, to their completed, cast-off time?
(To sell them would not be worth his while.)

In a letter of 4 October 1907 to his wife Rilke describes the contentment that
fills the small shops on the rue de Seine, and imagines the two of them enjoy-
ing it with their daughter: "Ah, if only that sufficed: I've sometimes had the
wish to buy myself a full shop window like that and sit myself down behind it
with a dog for twenty years. In the evening there would be light in the back
room, in front everything completely dark, and the three of us would sit and
eat, behind; I've noticed how, seen from the street, that always looks like a Last
Supper, so grand and ceremonious through the dark space. (This way,
though, one always has to contend with all the worries, the great ones and the
small ones.) . . ."

Die Brandstätte

Gemieden von dem Frühherbstmorgen, der
mißtrauisch war, lag hinter den versengten
Hauslinden, die das Heidehaus beengten,
ein Neues, Leeres. Eine Stelle mehr,

auf welcher Kinder, von Gott weiß woher,
einander zuschrien und nach Fetzen haschten.
Doch alle wurden stille, sooft er,
der Sohn von hier, aus heißen, halbveraschten

Gebälken Kessel und verbogne Tröge
an einem langen Gabelaste zog,—
um dann mit einem Blick als ob er löge
die andern anzusehn, die er bewog

zu glauben, was an dieser Stelle stand.
Denn seit es nicht mehr war, schien es ihm so
seltsam: phantastischer als Pharao.
Und er war anders. Wie aus fernem Land.

The Site of the Fire

Avoided by the early autumn morning,
which was mistrustful, behind the scorched
lime trees that cramped the heath-house,
lay a newness, an emptiness. One place more

upon which children, God knows from where,
screamed at one another and snatched at rags.
Yet they all stopped shouting whenever he,
the son from here, with a long forked bough

fished out kettles and twisted washtubs
from under hot, half-incinerated beams,—
and then, with the look of someone lying,
gazed at the others, whom he induced

to believe what stood upon that place.
For now that it was gone, it seemed to him
so strange: more fantastic than Pharaoh.
And he was different. As from a far-off land.

Die Gruppe

Paris

Als pflückte einer rasch zu einem Strauß:
ordnet der Zufall hastig die Gesichter,
lockert sie auf und drückt sie wieder dichter,
ergreift zwei ferne, läßt ein nahes aus,

tauscht das mit dem, bläst irgendeines frisch,
wirft einen Hund, wie Kraut, aus dem Gemisch
und zieht, was niedrig schaut, wie durch verworrne
Stiele und Blätter, an dem Kopf nach vorne

und bindet es ganz klein am Rande ein;
und streckt sich wieder, ändert und verstellt
und hat nur eben Zeit, zum Augenschein

zurückzuspringen mitten auf die Matte,
auf der im nächsten Augenblick der glatte
Gewichteschwinger seine Schwere schwellt.

The Group

Paris

As if one swiftly plucked for a bouquet:
Chance hastily arranges all the faces,
loosens them and clasps them even tighter,
grabs two distant ones, leaves a near one out,

swaps this for that, blows life into one drooping,
throws a dog from the mixture like a weed,
pulls what looks too low headfirst as if
through tangled leaves and stems up toward the front

and binds it in, minuscule, at the edge;
and stretches once more, alters and adjusts
and for inspection has just time enough

to spring back to the middle of the mat,
on which in the next instant the glistening
heavyweight swells with all his strength.

Schlangen-Beschwörung

Wenn auf dem Markt, sich wiegend, der Beschwörer
die Kürbisflöte pfeift, die reizt und lullt,
so kann es sein, daß er sich einen Hörer
herüberlockt, der ganz aus dem Tumult

der Buden eintritt in den Kreis der Pfeife,
die will und will und will und die erreicht,
daß das Reptil in seinem Korb sich steife
und die das steife schmeichlerisch erweicht,

abwechselnd immer schwindelnder und blinder
mit dem, was schreckt und streckt, und dem, was löst—;
und dann genügt ein Blick: so hat der Inder
dir eine Fremde eingeflößt,

in der du stirbst. Es ist als überstürze
glühender Himmel dich. Es geht ein Sprung
durch dein Gesicht. Es legen sich Gewürze
auf deine nordische Erinnerung,

die dir nichts hilft. Dich feien keine Kräfte,
die Sonne gärt, das Fieber fällt und trifft;
von böser Freude steilen sich die Schäfte,
und in den Schlangen glänzt das Gift.

Snake-Charming

When in the marketplace, swaying, the charmer
pipes on the gourd-flute that lulls and rouses,
it sometimes happens that he lures himself
a hearer, who crosses from the tumult

of the stalls into the circle of the pipe,
which wills and wills and wills until at last
it makes the reptile stiffen in its basket,
and fawns upon the stiffness till it softens,

alternating ever more dizzyingly and blindly
what startles and stretches with what unloosens—;
and then just a glance: and the Indian's
infused in you a foreignness,

in which you die. It's as though a blazing
sky crashed in on you. A crack
runs through your face. Spices pile themselves
upon your Nordic memory,

which is of no avail. No power's a charm,
the sun ferments, the fever falls and strikes;
the shafts rise up with malicious joy,
and poison glistens in the snakes.

Schwartze Katze

Ein Gespenst ist noch wie eine Stelle,
dran dein Blick mit einem Klange stößt;
aber da, an diesem schwarzen Felle
wird dein stärkstes Schauen aufgelöst:

wie ein Tobender, wenn er in vollster
Raserei ins Schwarze stampft,
jählings am benehmenden Gepolster
einer Zelle aufhört und verdampft.

Alle Blicke, die sie jemals trafen,
scheint sie also an sich zu verhehlen,
um darüber drohend und verdrossen
zuzuschauern und damit zu schlafen.
Doch auf einmal kehrt sie, wie geweckt,
ihr Gesicht und mitten in das deine:
und da triffst du deinen Blick im geelen
Amber ihrer runden Augensteine
unerwartet wieder: eingeschlossen
wie ein ausgestorbenes Insekt.

Black Cat

Even a ghost is like a place
your glance bumps into with a sound;
but here, when it encounters this black fur,
your strongest gaze will be dissolved:

the way a madman, when he in fullest
rage pounds into the blackness,
stops abruptly at the sponge-like padding
of a cell and drains away.

All the glances that have ever struck her
she seems to conceal upon herself
so that she can look them over,
morose and menacing, and sleep with them.
But all at once, as if awakened,
she turns her face straight into your own:
and you unexpectedly meet your gaze
in the yellow amber of her round eye-stones:
closed in like some long-extinct insect.

Vor-Ostern

Neapel

Morgen wird in diesen tiefgekerbten
Gassen, die sich durch getürmtes Wohnen
unten dunkel nach dem Hafen drängen,
hell das Gold der Prozessionen rollen;
statt der Fetzen werden die ererbten
Bettbezüge, welche wehen wollen,
von den immer höheren Balkonen
(wie in Fließendem gespiegelt) hängen.

Aber heute hämmert an den Klopfern
jeden Augenblick ein voll Bepackter,
und sie schleppen immer neue Käufe;
dennoch stehen strotzend noch die Stände.
An der Ecke zeigt ein aufgehackter
Ochse seine frischen Innenwände,
und in Fähnchen enden alle Läufe.
Und ein Vorrat wie von tausend Opfern

drängt auf Bänken, hängt sich rings um Pflöcke,
zwängt sich, wölbt sich, wälzt sich aus dem Dämmer
aller Türen, und vor dem Gegähne
der Melonen strecken sich die Brote.
Voller Gier und Handlung ist das Tote;
doch viel stiller sind die jungen Hähne
und die abgehängten Ziegenböcke
und am allerleisesten die Lämmer,

Easter Eve

Naples

Tomorrow in these deeply carved-out
streets, which below through piled-up living
press darkly toward the harbor,
brightly the procession's gold will roll;
instead of the rags the inherited
bed-covers, which want to wave,
will from the ever higher balconies
(as if endlessly reflected) hang.

But today someone loaded up with goods
pounds every moment on the doors,
and they keep lugging in new purchases;
even so, the stalls still stand there bursting.
On the corner an ox hacked wide apart
displays its glistening innards,
and all its legs end in little flags.
And a supply as from a thousand sacrifices

crowds on benches, clings around pegs,
squeezes, arches, spills out from the half-light
of every door, while the loaves stretch
before the yawning of the melons.
What's dead is full of lust and action;
yet much calmer are the cockerels
and the well-hung billy goats,
and gentlest of all are the lambs,

die die Knaben um die Schultern nehmen
und die willig von den Schritten nicken;
während in der Mauer der verglasten
spanischen Madonna die Agraffe
und das Silber in den Diademen
von dem Lichter-Vorgefühl beglänzter
schimmert. Aber drüber in dem Fenster
zeigt sich blickverschwenderisch ein Affe
und führt rasch in einer angemaßten
Haltung Gesten aus, die sich nicht schicken.

whom the boys wrap around their shoulders,
and who nod agreeably to their steps;
while in the wall of the glassed-in
Spanish Madonna the jeweled brooches
and the silver in the diadems
gleam more intensely with presentiment
of light. But in the window above
a glance-squandering monkey flaunts himself,
and, striking an insolent mimic pose,
swiftly pulls off gestures that just won't do.

Der Balkon

Neapel

Von der Enge, oben, des Balkones
angeordnet wie von einem Maler
und gebunden wie zu einem Strauß
alternder Gesichter und ovaler,
klar im Abend, sehn sie idealer,
rührender und wie für immer aus.

Diese aneinander angelehnten
Schwestern, die, als ob sie sich von weit
ohne Aussicht nacheinander sehnten,
lehnen, Einsamkeit an Einsamkeit;

und der Bruder mit dem feierlichen
Schweigen, zugeschlossen, voll Geschick,
doch von einem sanften Augenblick
mit der Mutter unbemerkt verglichen;

und dazwischen, abgelebt und länglich,
längst mit keinem mehr verwandt,
einer Greisin Maske, unzugänglich,
wie im Fallen von der einen Hand

aufgehalten, während eine zweite
welkere, als ob sie weitergleite,
unten vor den Kleidern hängt zur Seite

von dem Kinder-Angesicht,
das das Letzte ist, versucht, verblichen,
von den Stäben wieder durchgestrichen
wie noch unbestimmbar, wie noch nicht.

The Balcony

Naples

Arranged, up above, by the balcony's
constrictedness as by a painter
and bound as if to make a bouquet
of aging and tightly oval faces,
bright in the dusk, they look more ideal,
more touching, and as if for ever.

These sisters propped against each other,
who, as though they from far away
without prospect yearned for one another,
lean, solitude on solitude;

and the brother with his solemn
silence, locked up, full of destiny,
yet by an unobtrusive moment
compared, unnoticed, with the mother;

and in between, gaunt and drawn out,
long since unrelated to the rest,
an old woman's mask, inapproachable,
as if stopped in mid-fall

by the one hand, while a second
more withered one, as if it glided on,
hangs below in front of her dress

to the side of the child-countenance,
which is the last of them, tried, faded,
crossed out again by the bars, as if
still indefinable, still deferred.

Auswanderer-Schiff

Neapel

Denk: daß einer heiß und glühend flüchte,
und die Sieger wären hinterher,
und auf einmal machte der
Flüchtende kurz, unerwartet, Kehr
gegen Hunderte—: so sehr
warf sich das Erglühende der Früchte
immer wieder an das blaue Meer:

als das langsame Orangen-Boot
sie voübertrug bis an das große
graue Schiff, zu dem, von Stoß zu Stoße,
andre Boote Fische hoben, Brot,—
während es, voll Hohn, in seinmen Schooße
Kohlen aufnahm, offen wie der Tod.

Emigrant-Ship

Naples

Imagine: that someone fled hot and burning,
and the victors were close behind,
and all at once the fleeing one turned,
abrupt, unexpected, and charged
against hundreds—: that intensely
the glow of all the fruit threw itself
again and again at the blue sea:

as the slow-moving orange-boat
carried them past, on out to the huge
gray ship, into which, from thrust to thrust,
other boats were lifting fish, bread,—
while it, full of scorn, took
coal into its womb, open like death.

Landschaft

Wie zuletzt, in einem Augenblick
aufgehäuft aus Hängen, Häusern, Stücken
alter Himmel und zerbrochnen Brücken,
und von drüben her, wie vom Geschick,
von dem Sonnenuntergang getroffen,
angeschuldigt, aufgerissen, offen—
ginge dort die Ortschaft tragisch aus:

fiele nicht auf einmal in das Wunde,
drin zerfließend, aus der nächsten Stunde
jener Tropfen kühlen Blaus,
der die Nacht schon in den Abend mischt,
so daß das von ferne Angefachte
sachte, wie erlöst, erlischt.

Ruhig sind die Tore und die Bogen,
durchsichtige Wolken wogen
über blassen Häuserreihn
die schon Dunkel in sich eingesogen;
aber plötzlich ist vom Mond ein Schein
durchgeglitten, licht, als hätte ein
Erzengel irgendwo sein Schwert gezogen.

Landscape

How at last, in an instant
heaped up out of houses, slopes,
pieces of old sky and broken bridges,
and struck, as if by destiny,
from over there by the setting sun,
accused, torn open, exposed—
that village would go out tragically:

if suddenly there didn't fall into
the wound, melting in it, from the next hour
that drop of cool blue, which already
blends the night into the evening,
so that what was inflamed from far away
dies out softly, as if saved.

The gates and the arches are peaceful,
transparent cloud banks surge
over pale rows of houses
that have already soaked up darkness;
but suddenly from the moon a gleam
has glided through, bright, as if somewhere
an archangel had unsheathed his sword.

Römische Campagna

Aus der vollgestellten Stadt, die lieber
schliefe, träumend von den hohen Thermen,
geht der grade Gräberweg ins Fieber;
und die Fenster in den letzten Fermen

sehn ihm nach mit einem bösen Blick.
Und er hat sie immer im Genick,
wenn er hingeht, rechts und links zerstörend,
bis er draußen atemlos beschwörend

seine Leere zu den Himmeln hebt,
hastig um sich schauend, ob ihn keine
Fenster treffen. Während er den weiten

Aquädukten zuwinkt herzuschreiten,
geben ihm die Himmel für die seine
ihre Leere, die ihn überlebt.

Roman Campagna

From the cluttered city, which would rather
sleep, dreaming of the splendid Thermae,
the tomb-road heads straight for the fever,
and the windows in the last farms

follow after it with an evil eye.
And it has them always at its neck
as it goes past, destroying left and right,
until outside, breathlessly beseeching,

it lifts its emptiness up to the skies,
quickly looking all around it, to see
if any window watches. While it signals

to the far aqueducts to stride closer,
the skies take away its emptiness
and give it their own, which will outlive it.

Roman Campagna: The Appian Way, ancient high road leading from Rome to
lower Italy, and eventually entering the Pontine Marshes (hence, probably,
the obscure *ins Fieber* of line 3). The ruins of the magnificent thermae, or
baths, of Caracalla, are the last important building it passes before it leaves the
city, and tombs line its passage through the countryside.

Lied vom Meer

Capri. Piccola Marina

Uraltes Wehn vom Meer,
Meerwind bei Nacht:
    du kommst zu keinem her;
wenn einer wacht,
so muß er sehn, wie er
dich übersteht:
    uraltes Wehn vom Meer,
welches weht
nur wie für Ur-Gestein,
lauter Raum
reißend von weit herein . . .

O wie fühlt dich ein
treibender Feigenbaum
oben im Mondschein.

Song from the Sea

Capri, Piccola Marina

Age-old breeze from the sea,
sea wind by night:
    you come seeking no one;
whoever wakes
must find his own way
to outlast you;
    age-old breeze from the sea,
blowing only
as if for age-old stone,
sheer space
tearing in from afar . . .

O how you're felt by
a burgeoning fig tree
high in the moonlight.

Nächtliche Fahrt

Sankt Petersburg

Damals als wir mit den glatten Trabern
(schwarzen, aus dem Orloff'schen Gestüt)—,
während hinter hohen Kandelabern
Stadtnachtfronten lagen, angefrüht,
stumm und keiner Stunde mehr gemäß—,
fuhren, nein: vergingen oder flogen
und um lastende Paläste bogen
in das Wehn der Newa-Quais,

hingerissen durch das wache Nachten,
das nicht Himmel und nicht Erde hat,—
als das Drängende von unbewachten
Gärten gärend aus dem Ljetnij-Ssad
aufstieg, während seine Steinfiguren
schwindend mit ohnmächtigen Konturen
hinter uns vergingen, wie wir fuhren—:

damals hörte diese Stadt
auf zu sein. Auf einmal gab sie zu,
daß sie niemals war, um nichts als Ruh
flehend; wie ein Irrer, dem das Wirrn
plötzlich sich entwirrt, das ihn verriet,
und der einen jahrelangen kranken
gar nicht zu verwandelnden Gedanken,
den er nie mehr denken muß: Granit—
aus dem leeren schwankenden Gehirn
fallen fühlt, bis man ihn nicht mehr sieht.

Night Drive

St. Petersburg

That time, when drawn by the sleek trotters
(black ones, sired by an Orlov stud)—,
while behind tall street lamps
city-night facades stood, tinged with dawn,
mute, no longer fitted to an hour—,
we were driving, no: disappearing or flying
and bending around ponderous palaces
into the wind of the Neva-Quay,

transported through the wakeful night
that hasn't sky and hasn't earth,—
as the clamoring of unattended gardens
rose up seething from the Letney-Sad
while its stone statues, dwindling
impotently with unconscious contours,
disappeared behind us as we drove—:

that time this city ceased
to be. It all at once admitted
that it never was, begging only peace;
like a lunatic, when the confusion
that betrayed him suddenly unravels,
and he feels a sickly years-long
utterly unalterable thought
he never has to think again: granite—
fall from his empty reeling brain
until it vanishes from sight.

l. 12, *Ljetnij-Ssad*: a large park (lit. "Summer Garden") belonging to the Czars.

Papageien-Park

Jardin des Plantes, Paris

Unter türkischen Linden, die blühen, an Rasenrändern,
in leise von ihrem Heimweh geschaukelten Ständern
atmen die Ara und wissen von ihren Ländern,
die sich, auch wenn sie nicht hinsehn, nicht verändern.

Fremd im beschäftigten Grünen wie eine Parade,
zieren sie sich und fühlen sich selber zu schade,
und mit den kostbaren Schnäbeln aus Jaspis und Jade
kauen sie Graues, verschleudern es, finden es fade.

Unten klauben die duffen Tauben, was sie nicht mögen,
während sich oben die höhnischen Vögel verbeugen
zwischen den beiden fast leeren vergeudeten Trögen.

Aber dann wiegen sie wieder und schläfern und äugen,
spielen mit dunkelen Zungen, die gerne lögen,
zerstreut an den Fußfesselringen. Warten auf Zeugen.

Parrot-Park

Jardin des Plantes, Paris

Under blossoming Turkish lindens, at grassy verges,
in stands rocked gently by their languishings for home,
the Aras breathe and think about their countries,
which, even though their eyes aren't on them, never alter.

As out of place within this busy green as a parade,
they put on airs and feel themselves to be above it all,
and with those precious beaks made out of jade and jasper
chew a gray something, find it tasteless, toss it away.

Down below the dreary doves pick up what they've disdained,
while from above the scornful birds make a mock-obeisant bow
between their two squandered, nearly empty feeding-trays.

But then they start rocking again and sleeping and watching,
and with dark tongues, which would gladly tell lies, play
distractedly with their foot-chains. Waiting for witnesses.

Die Parke

Unaufhaltsam heben sich die Parke
aus dem sanft zerfallenden Vergehn;
überhäuft mit Himmeln, überstarke
Überlieferte, die überstehn,

um sich auf den klaren Rasenplänen
auszubreiten und zurückzuziehn,
immer mit demselben souveränen
Aufwand, wie beschützt durch ihn,

und den unerschöpflichen Erlös
königlicher Größe noch vermehrend,
aus sich steigend, in sich wiederkehrend:
huldvoll, prunkend, purpurn und pompös.

The Parks

I
Irresistibly the parks rise up
from the softly decomposing transience;
heaped with heavens, superstrong
traditions, which overcome

in order on the clear grassy plots
to spread out and withdraw themselves,
always with the same sovereign
extravagance, as if protected by it,

and still adding to the endless
profits that accrue to royal greatness,
rising from themselves, returning to themselves:
resplendent, crimson, gracious, grandiose.

II
Leise von den Alleen
ergriffen, rechts und links,
folgend dem Weitergehen
irgend eines Winks,

trittst du mit einem Male
in das Beisammensein
einer schattigen Wasserschale
mit vier Bänken aus Stein;

in eine abgetrennte
Zeit, die allein vergeht.
Auf feuchte Postamente,
auf denen nichts mehr steht,

hebst du einen tiefen
erwartenden Atemzug;
während das silberne Triefen
von dem dunkeln Bug

dich schon zu den Seinen
zählt und weiterspricht.
Und du fühlst dich unter Steinen
die hören, und rührst dich nicht.

II

Gently gripped by the
avenues, left and right,
led by the beckoning
of some persistent wave,

you step all of a sudden
into the meeting place
of a shadowed water basin
and four stone benches;

in a separated time
that dwindles past alone.
On damp marble bases
where nothing any longer stands,

you raise a deep
expectant breath;
while the silver dripping
from the dark basin

already counts you among
its own and talks on.
And feeling yourself among stones
that listen, you don't stir.

III

Den Teichen und den eingerahmten Weihern
verheimlicht man noch immer das Verhör
der Könige. Sie warten unter Schleiern,
und jeden Augenblick kann Monseigneur

vorüberkommen; und dann wollen sie
des Königs Laune oder Trauer mildern
und von den Marmorrändern wieder die
Teppiche mit alten Spiegelbildern

hinunterhängen, wie um einen Platz:
auf grünem Grund, mit Silber, Rosa, Grau,
gewährtem Weiß und leicht gerührtem Blau
und einem Könige und einer Frau
und Blumen in dem wellenden Besatz.

III
The pools and the framed fish ponds are still
not told about the interrogation
of the king. They wait beneath veils,
and at any moment the Dauphin

can pass their way; and then they want
to mollify the king's mood or sorrow
and from their marble edges again let
the tapestries with old reflections

hang down, as if around a square:
on green ground, with gray, silver, rose,
granted white and easily moved blue
and a king and a woman
and flowers in the rippling border.

IV
Und Natur, erlaucht und als verletze
sie nur unentschloßnes Ungefähr,
nahm von diesen Königen Gesetze,
selber selig, um den Tapis-vert

ihrer Bäume Traum and Übertreibung
aufzutürmen aus gebauschtem Grün
und die Abende nach der Beschreibung
von Verliebten in die Avenün

einzumalen mit dem weichen Pinsel,
der ein firnisklares aufgelöstes
Lächeln glänzend zu enthalten schien:

der Natur ein liebes, nicht ihr größtes,
aber eines, das sie selbst verliehn,
um auf rosenvoller Liebes-Insel
es zu einem größern aufzuziehn.

IV

And Nature, augustly, as if only
weak-willed impreciseness offended her,
accepted laws from kings like these,
herself in bliss, that she might stack up

her trees' dreams and exaggerations
into that tapis-vert of billowed green
and paint, according to how lovers
have described them, the evening shades,

into the tree-lined walks, with that soft brush
which seemed to sparkle inwardly
with a varnish-clear, unfettered smile:

one dear to Nature, not her most distinguished,
but a smile that she herself gave out,
to have it grow up to some higher purpose
on a rose-filled isle of love.

v

Götter von Alleen und Altanen,
niemals ganzgeglaubte Götter, die
altern in den gradbeschnittnen Bahnen,
höchstens angelächelte Dianen
wenn die königliche Venerie

wie ein Wind die hohen Morgen teilend
aufbrach, übereilt und übereilend—;
höchstens angelächelte, doch nie

angeflehte Götter. Elegante
Pseudonyme, unter denen man
sich verbarg und blühte oder brannte,—
leichtgeneigte, lächelnd angewandte
Götter, die noch manchmal dann und wann

Das gewähren, was sie einst gewährten,
wenn das Blühen der entzückten Gärten
ihnen ihre kalte Haltung nimmt;
wenn sie ganz von ersten Schatten beben
und Versprechen um Versprechen geben,
alle unbegrenzt und unbestimmt.

v

Gods of avenues and balconies,
never quite believed-in gods, who
grow old in the straight-clipped thoroughfares,
Dianas who at most were smiled upon
when the royal hunt broke out

like a wind dividing the tall morning,
heedless and precipitate—;
at most smiled-upon, but never

entreated gods. Elegant pseudonyms
under which one hid and burned or blossomed,—
easily inclined, smilingly employed
gods, who still sometimes now and then

grant that which they once granted,
when the blossoming of delighted gardens
takes their cold bearing away from them;
when they tremble all over from first shadows
and give promise after promise,
all so limitless and indistinct.

VI

Fühlst du, wie keiner von allen
Wegen steht und stockt;
von gelassenen Treppen fallen,
durch ein Nichts von Neigung
leise weitergelockt,
über alle Terrassen
die Wege, zwischen den Massen
verlangsamt und gelenkt,
bis zu den weiten Teichen,
wo sie (wie einem Gleichen)
der reiche Park verschenkt

an den reichen Raum: den Einen,
der mit Scheinen und Widerscheinen
seinen Besitz durchdringt,
aus dem er von allen Seiten
Weiten mit sich bringt,
wenn er aus schließenden Weihern
zu wolkigen Abendfeiern
sich in die Himmel schwingt.

VI
Do you feel how none of all these
pathways stands and stagnates;
from serene steps falling,
through the merest trace of slope
gently lured on,
over all the terraces
the pathways, between the masses
slowed down and steered,
on out to the distant pools,
where (as to an equal)
the rich park gives them

to the rich space: the space
that with light and light's reflections
completely saturates its realm,
and from that bright estate
brings distances on every side
when from closing fish ponds
toward cloud-filled evening fêtes
it vaults into the sky.

Aber Schalen sind, drin der Najaden
Spiegelbilder, die sie nicht mehr baden,
wie ertrunken liegen, sehr verzerrt;
die Alleen sind durch Balustraden
in der Ferne wie versperrt.

Immer geht ein feuchter Blätterfall
durch die Luft hinunter wie auf Stufen,
jeder Vogelruf ist wie verrufen,
wie vergiftet jede Nachtigall.

Selbst der Frühling ist da nicht mehr gebend,
diese Büsche glauben nicht an ihn;
ungern duftet trübe, überlebend
abgestandener Jasmin

alt und mit Zerfallendem vermischt.
Mit dir weiter rückt ein Bündel Mücken,
so als würde hinter deinem Rücken
alles gleich vernichtet und verwischt.

VII

But there are bowls in which the Naiads'
reflections, no longer being bathed,
lie as if drowned, all twisted out of shape;
the avenues are closed by balustrades
in the distance as if barred.

A damp leaf-fall descends forever
through the air, as if on steps;
every bird's cry is as if notorious,
as if poisoned every nightingale.

Even spring is no longer lavish here,
these bushes don't believe in it;
grudgingly the gloomy, half-surviving
dried-up jasmine puts forth a stale fragrance

mingled with decay. As you walk along,
a swarm of gnats moves with you, as though
behind your back everything were being
instantly annihilated and erased.

Bildnis

Dass von dem verzichtenden Gesichte
keiner ihrer großen Schmerzen fiele,
trägt sie langsam durch die Trauerspiele
ihrer Züge schönen welken Strauß,
wild gebunden und schon beinah lose;
manchmal fällt, wie eine Tuberose,
ein verlornes Lächeln müd heraus.

Und sie geht gelassen drüber hin,
müde, mit den schönen blinden Händen,
welche wissen, daß sie es nicht fänden,—

und sie sagt Erdichtetes, darin
Schicksal schwankt, gewolltes, irgendeines,
und sie giebt ihm ihrer Seele Sinn,
daß es ausbricht wie ein Ungemeines:
wie das Schreien eines Steines—

und sie läßt, mit hochgehobnem Kinn,
alle diese Worte wieder fallen,
ohne bleibend; denn nicht eins von allen
ist der wehen Wirklichkeit gemäß,
ihrem einzigen Eigentum,
das sie, wie ein fußloses Gefäß,
halten muß, hoch über ihren Ruhm
und den Gang der Abende hinaus.

Portrait

That from her face of absolute refusal
not one of her great sorrows might fall,
she carries slowly through the tragedies
her features' beautiful faded bouquet,
wildly tied and already coming loose;
sometimes a lost smile, like a tuberose,
falls from it wearily and drifts down.

And she goes by with serene indifference,
weary, with the beautiful blind hands,
which know that they would never find it,—

and she says fabricated things, in which
fate wavers, forced, fit for anyone,
and she gives it her own soul's meaning,
so that it breaks out like something fabulous:
like the screaming of a stone—

and she lets, with high uplifted chin,
all these phrases fall again,
staying without any; for not a one
is worthy of that sad reality,
her sole possession,
which she, like a footless vessel,
must hold out, high above her fame
and the way each evening goes.

Venezianischer Morgen

Richard Beer-Hofmann zugeeignet

Fürstlich verwöhnte Fenster sehen immer,
was manchesmal uns zu bemühn geruht:
die Stadt, die immer wieder, wo ein Schimmer
von Himmel trifft auf ein Gefühl von Flut,

sich bildet ohne irgendwann zu sein.
Ein jeder Morgen muß ihr die Opale
erst zeigen, die sie gestern trug, und Reihn
von Spiegelbildern ziehn aus dem Kanale
und sie erinnern an die andern Male:
dann giebt sie sich erst zu und fällt sich ein

wie eine Nymphe, die den Zeus empfing.
Das Ohrgehäng erklingt an ihrem Ohre;
sie aber hebt San Giorgio Maggiore
und lächelt lässig in das schöne Ding.

Venetian Morning

Dedicated to Richard Beer-Hofmann

Windows pampered like princes see always
what now and then deigns to trouble us:
the city that, time and again, where a shimmer
of sky strikes a feeling of floodtide,

takes shape without once choosing to be.
Each new morning must first show her
the opals she wore yesterday, and pull
rows of reflections out of the canal
and remind her of all the other times:
only then does she concede and settle in

like a nymph who received Zeus.
The dangling earrings ring out at her ear;
but she lifts San Giorgio Maggiore
and smiles idly into that lovely thing.

Spätherbst in Venedig

Nun treibt die Stadt schon nicht mehr wie ein Köder,
der alle aufgetauchten Tage fängt.
Die gläsernen Paläste klingen spröder
an deinen Blick. Und aus den Gärten hängt

der Sommer wie ein Haufen Marionetten
kopfüber, müde, umgebracht.
Aber vom Grund aus alten Waldskeletten
steigt Willen auf: als sollte über Nacht

der General des Meeres die Galeeren
verdoppeln in dem wachen Arsenal,
um schon die nächste Morgenluft zu teeren

mit einer Flotte, welche ruderschlagend
sich drängt und jäh, mit allen Flaggen tagend,
den großen Wind hat, strahlend und fatal.

Late Autumn in Venice

Already the city no longer drifts
like a bait, catching the days as they surface.
The glassy palaces ring more brittly
against your gaze. And from the gardens

the summer hangs like a heap of marionettes,
headfirst, exhausted, done in.
But from the ground, out of old forest skeletons,
volition rises: as if overnight

the commander of the sea had to double
the galleys in the sleepless arsenal,
in order to tar the next morning breeze

with a fleet, which pushes out rowing
and then suddenly, with all its flags dawning,
has the great wind, radiant and dire.

San Marco
Venedig

In diesem Innern, das wie ausgehöhlt
sich wölbt und wendet in den goldnen Smalten,
rundkantig, glatt, mit Köstlichkeit geölt,
ward dieses Staates Dunkelheit gehalten

und heimlich aufgehäuft, als Gleichgewicht
des Lichtes, das in allen seinen Dingen
sich so vermehrte, daß sie fast vergingen—.
Und plötzlich zweifelst du: vergehn sie nicht?

und drängst zurück die harte Galerie,
die, wie ein Gang im Bergwerk, nah am Glanz
der Wölbung hängt; und du erkennst die heile

Helle des Ausblicks: aber irgendwie
wehmütig messend ihre müde Weile
am nahen Überstehn des Viergespanns.

San Marco

Venice

In this interior, which turns and arches
inside the golden cobalt like a cave,
round-cornered, sleek, oiled with exquisiteness,
this state's darkness was retained

and secretly piled up, as counterbalance
to the light that so increased
in all its things, they almost perished—.
And suddenly it strikes you: don't they perish?

and you force back the hard gallery
that hangs like a passage in a mine
near the dome's brilliance: and you recognize

the bright prospect, still intact: yet somehow
wistfully compare its tired interim
with the proud enduring of the team-of-four.

l. 14, *Viergespann*: lit., a four-in-hand or quadriga. The reference is almost certainly to the four bronze horses of San Marco, treasures of antiquity that stand high over the central porch of the west front of St. Mark's. They were brought to Venice from Constantinople in 1204, as part of the plunder when that city was taken in the Fourth Crusade.

Ein Doge

Fremde Gesandte sahen, wie sie geizten
mit ihm und allem was er tat;
während sie ihn zu seiner Größe reizten,
umstellten sie das goldene Dogat

mit Spähern und Beschränkern immer mehr,
bange, daß nicht die Macht sie überfällt,
die sie in ihm (so wie man Löwen hält)
vorsichtig nährten. Aber er,

im Schutze seiner halbverhängten Sinne,
ward dessen nicht gewahr und hielt nicht inne,
größer zu werden. Was die Signorie

in seinem Innern zu bezwingen glaubte,
bezwang er selbst. In seinem greisen Haupte
war es besiegt. Sein Antlitz zeigte wie.

A Doge

Foreign envoys saw how miserly they were
with him and with everything he did;
for while they pricked him on to greatness,
they hedged the golden dogacy about

with more and more lookouts and restricters,
afraid they'd be asaulted by the might
which they in him (the way men keep lions)
were feeding cautiously. But he,

under cover of his half-veiled senses,
took no note of that and kept on
growing greater. What the Signorie

thought to conquer in his inmost being,
he himself conquered. In his wizened head
it was defeated. His face showed how.

Die Laute

Ich bin die Laute. Willst du meinen Leib
beschreiben, seine schön gewölbten Streifen:
sprich so, als sprächest du von einer reifen
gewölbten Feige. Übertreib

das Dunkel, das du in mir siehst. Es war
Tullias Dunkelheit. In ihrer Scham
war nicht so viel, und ihr erhelltes Haar
war wie ein heller Saal. Zuweilen nahm

sie etwas Klang von meiner Oberfläche
in ihr Gesicht und sang zu mir.
Dann spannte ich mich gegen ihre Schwäche,
und endlich war mein Inneres in ihr.

The Lute

I am the lute. If you wish to describe
my body, with its beautiful arching stripes:
speak of me as you would of a ripe
full-bodied fig. Exaggerate

the darkness that you see in me. It was
Tullia's darkness. In her most private place
there wasn't so much, and her bright hair
was like a light-filled hall. Sometimes

she took some sound from my surface
into her face and sang while I played.
Then I tensed myself against her yielding,
until at last my inmost self was in her.

l. 6, *Tullia*: most commentators suggest Tullia d'Aragona, a famous courtesan
(as well as poet and musician) of sixteenth-century Italy. But a still more fa-
mous "Tullia" is Cicero's daughter, whose body, according to legend, was
found after 1500 years in a monument along the Appian way, with a lamp still
burning there, before contact with the air turned both to dust. (Donne alludes
to the legend, and to "Tullia" by name, in one of his epithalamiums.) The
name should probably be allowed its mystery. It evokes an intimacy and a
lived dimension that exclude us; in doing so it underscores the lute's inacces-
sibility, both as historical artifact and as Rilkean "thing."

Der Abenteuerer

I

Wenn er unter jene welche *waren*
trat: der Plötzliche, der *schien*,
was ein Glanz wie von Gefahren
in dem augesparten Raum um ihn,

den er lächelnd überschritt, um einer
Herzogin den Fächer aufzuheben:
diesen warmen Fächer, den er eben
wollte fallen sehen. Und wenn keiner

mit ihm eintrat in die Fensternische
(wo die Parke gleich ins Träumerische
stiegen, wenn er nur nach ihnen wies),
ging er lässig an die Kartentische
und gewann. Und unterließ

nicht, die Blicke alle zu behalten,
die ihn zweifelnd oder zärtlich trafen,
und auch die in Spiegel fielen, galten.
Er beschloß, auch heute nicht zu schlafen

wie die letzte lange Nacht, und bog
einen Blick mit seinem rücksichtslosen
welcher war: als hätte er von Rosen
Kinder, die man irgendwo erzog.

The Adventurer

I

When among those who *were*
he moved: the sudden one, who *shone*,
a radiance as if from danger
filled the space left blank around him,

which he crossed over smiling, in order
to a duchess to lift up her fan:
this warm fan, which he had just been
wanting to see fall; and if no one

joined him inside the window-niche
(where the parks rose into the dreamlike
when he no more than gestured toward them),
he walked carelessly to the card table
and won. And was not remiss

to save up all their glances, which struck him
with tenderness or edged with doubt;
even those cast into mirrors he collected.
He resolved not to sleep today as well

remembering the last long night, and bent
a glance with his own ruthless one
which was: as if it had by roses
children, who were being raised somewhere.

II

In den Tagen—(nein, es waren keine),
da die Flut sein unterstes Verlies
ihm bestritt, als wär es nicht das seine,
und ihn, steigend, an die Steine
der daran gewöhnten Wölbung stieß,

fiel ihm plötzlich einer von den Namen
wieder ein, die er vor Zeiten trug.
Und er wußte wieder: Leben kamen,
wenn er lockte; wie im Flug

kamen sie: noch warme Leben Toter,
die er, ungeduldiger, bedrohter,
weiterlebte mitten drin;
oder die nicht ausgelebten Leben,
und er wußte sie hinaufzuheben,
und sie hatten wieder Sinn.

Oft war keine Stelle an ihm sicher,
und er zitterte: Ich bin————
doch im nächsten Augenblicke glich er
dem Geliebten einer Königin.

Immer wieder war ein Sein zu haben:
die Geschicke angefangner Knaben,
die, als hätte man sie nicht gewagt,
abgebrochen waren, abgesagt,
nahm er auf und riß sie in sich hin;
denn er mußte einmal nur die Gruft
solcher Aufgegebener durchschreiten,
und die Düfte ihrer Möglichkeiten
lagen wieder in der Luft.

II

In those days—(no, there were no days),
when the floodtide challenged him his
lowest dungeon, as if it weren't his own,
and thrust him, rising, on the stones
that arched indifferently above it,

suddenly a name came back to him
from those which ages past he bore.
And he knew again: lives came,
when he lured: as if winging there

they came: still warm lives of dead,
which he, more impatiently, with greater danger,
went on living in its midst;
or lives not completely lived,
and he knew how to raise them up,
and they once more had meaning.

Often no place about him was secure,
and he trembled: I am————
yet in the next instant he was like
the favorite of a queen.

Always some new existence could be had:
the destinies of young boys scarcely started,
which—as if in fear of where they led—
had been cancelled, broken off,
he took up and ripped into himself;
for he only had to stride through once
the crypt of such surrendered lives,
and the fresh scent of their possibilities
was once again in the air.

Falken-Beize

Kaiser sein heißt unverwandelt vieles
überstehen bei geheimer Tat:
wenn der Kanzler nachts den Turm betrat,
fand er *ihn*, des hohen Federspieles
kühnen fürstlichen Traktat

in den eingeneigten Schreiber sagen;
denn er hatte im entlegnen Saale
selber nächtelang und viele Male
das noch ungewohnte Tier getragen,

wenn es fremd war, neu und aufgebräut.
Und er hatte dann sich nie gescheut,
Pläne, welche in ihm aufgesprungen,
oder zärtlicher Erinnerungen
tieftiefinneres Geläut
zu verachten, um des bangen jungen

Falken willen, dessen Blut und Sorgen
zu begreifen er sich nicht erließ.
Dafür war er auch wie mitgehoben,
wenn der Vogel, den die Herren loben,
glänzend von der Hand geworfen, oben
in dem mitgefühlten Frühlingsmorgen
wie ein Engel auf den Reiher stieß.

Falconry

Being Emperor means outlasting many
things unmoved, through action one keeps hidden:
when at night the chancellor stepped
into the tower, he found *him* there, saying
that bold princely tract on falconry

into a scribe bent in upon his words;
for he himself in that sequestered hall
had paced nights long and many times
with the unsettled creature on his arm,

when it was strange, new, and full of turbulence.
And whatever beckoned then—
plans which had sprung up in him,
or tender recollections'
deep, deep inner chiming—
he had spurned at once, for that frightened fledgling

falcon's sake, whose blood and worries
he taxed himself relentlessly to grasp.
In exchange he too seemed borne aloft,
when the bird, to whom the lords give praise,
tossed radiantly from his hand, above
in that all-embracing springtime morning
dropped like an angel on the heron.

The German Emperor Frederick II (1194–1250) and his treatise on falconry,
De arte venandi cum avibus.

Corrida

In memoriam Montez, 1830

Seit er, klein beinah, aus dem Toril
ausbrach, aufgescheuchten Augs und Ohrs,
und den Eigensinn des Picadors
und die Bänderhaken wie im Spiel

hinnahm, ist die stürmische Gestalt
angewachsen—sieh: zu welcher Masse,
aufgehäuft aus altem schwarzen Hasse,
und das Haupt zu einer Faust geballt,

nicht mehr spielend gegen irgendwen,
nein: die blutigen Nackenhaken hissend
hinter den gefällten Hörnern, wissend
und von Ewigkeit her gegen Den,

der in Gold und mauver Rosaseide
plötzlich umkehrt und, wie einen Schwarm
Bienen und als ob ers eben leide,
den Bestürzten unter seinem Arm

durchläßt,—während seine Blicke heiß
sich noch einmal heben, leichtgelenkt,
und als schlüge draußen jener Kreis
sich aus ihrem Glanz und Dunkel nieder
und aus jedem Schlagen seiner Lider,

ehe er gleichmütig, ungehässig,
an sich selbst gelehnt, gelassen, lässig
in die wiederhergerollte große
Woge über dem verlornen Stoße
seinen Degen beinah sanft versenkt.

Corrida

In Memoriam Montez, 1830

Since he, small almost, first broke
from the wooden gate, his eyes and ears
wide open, and took the stubborn proddings
of the picador and the ribboned hooks

as in a game, the turbulent form
has grown—look: into such a mass,
piled up out of ancient black hatred,
and the head clenched into a fist,

no longer darting at this man or that,
no: hoisting the bloody shoulder-hooks
behind his lowered horns, recognizing
and from eternity cast against Him,

who in his gold and mauve-pink silk
suddenly twists round, and, like a swarm
of bees, as if he simply suffered it,
lets the baffled animal through

beneath his arm,—while his burning eyes
look up once more, poised and agile,
as if that circle drifted down outside
from the action of their shine and darkness
and from each strong beating of his lids,

before he serenely, unspitefully,
leaning on himself, calmly, carelessly
into that great wave, turned round and once more
rolling toward him, above its lost thrust
almost gently sinks his sword.

Don Juans Kindheit

In seiner Schlankheit war, schon fast entscheidend,
der Bogen, der an Frauen nicht zerbricht;
und manchmal, seine Stirne nicht mehr meidend,
ging eine Neigung durch sein Angesicht

zu einer die vorüberkam, zu einer
die ihm ein fremdes altes Bild verschloß:
er lächelte. Er war nicht mehr der Weiner,
der sich ins Dunkel trug und sich vergoß.

Und während ein ganz neues Selbstvertrauen
ihn öfter tröstete und fast verzog,
ertrug er ernst den ganzen Blick der Frauen,
der ihn bewunderte und ihn bewog.

Don Juan's Childhood

In his slimness was the bow, already almost
taut, that no woman's pull could break;
and sometimes, no longer keeping to itself,
an inclination moved across his face

toward one of them who came past, toward one
from whom a strange ancient image barred him:
he smiled. He was no longer now the weeper
who bore himself into the dark and spilled himself.

And as a wholly new self-confidence
soothed more often and almost spoiled him,
he bore candidly the whole gaze of women,
which admired him and bent him to his will.

Don Juans Auswahl

Und der Engel trat ihn an: Bereite
dich mir ganz. Und da ist mein Gebot.
Denn daß einer jene überschreite,
die die Süßesten an ihrer Seite
bitter machen, tut mir not.
Zwar auch du kannst wenig besser lieben,
(unterbrich mich nicht: du irrst),
doch du glühest, und es steht geschrieben,
daß du viele führen wirst
zu der Einsamkeit, die diesen
tiefen Eingang hat. Laß ein
die, die ich dir zugewiesen,
daß sie wachsend Heloïsen
überstehn und überschrein.

Don Juan's Selection

And the Angel approached him: Give yourself
entirely to me. That's my command.
For I want someone to go beyond
those who make the sweetest
bitter at their sides. I know that at love
even you are scarcely any better,
(don't interrupt me: you're wrong),
yet you glow, and it is written
that you will lead many
to the solitude which has this
deep entrance. Let in
those whom I assign to you,
that growing they may
come through and cry past Heloise.

Sankt Georg

Und sie hatte ihn die ganze Nacht
angerufen, hingekniet, die schwache
wache Jungfrau: Siehe, dieser Drache,
und ich weiß es nicht, warum er wacht.

Und da brach er aus dem Morgengraun
auf dem Falben, strahlend Helm und Haubert,
und er sah sie, traurig und verzaubert
aus dem Knieen aufwärtsschaun

zu dem Glanze, der er war.
Und er sprengte glänzend längs der Länder
abwärts mit erhobnem Doppelhänder
in die offene Gefahr,

viel zu furchtbar, aber doch erfleht.
Und sie kniete knieender, die Hände
fester faltend, daß er sie bestände;
denn sie wußte nicht, daß Der besteht,

den ihr Herz, ihr reines und bereites,
aus dem Licht des göttlichen Geleites
niederreißt. Zuseiten seines Streites
stand, wie Türme stehen, ihr Gebet.

Saint George

And the whole night she had invoked his presence,
kneeling there, insistent, that frail
wakeful virgin: Look, this coiled dragon,
and I don't know why he keeps awake.

And then he broke from the morning haze
on the dun horse, with helm and hauberk blazing,
and he saw her, deep in her kneeling,
gazing up sad and spellbound

at that radiance, which he was.
And he charged radiantly the length of nations
down with raised two-handed sword
into the open peril,

far too dreadful, and yet implored.
And she knelt more fervently, her hands
folding tighter, that he might come through it;
for she didn't know, that He endures,

whom her heart, her pure and ready heart,
tears down out of the light that holds
the heavenly ranks. Alongside his battle
stood, the way towers stand, her prayer.

Dame auf einem Balkon

Plötzlich tritt sie, in den Wind gehüllt,
licht in Lichtes, wie herausgegriffen,
während jetzt die Stube wie geschliffen
hinter ihr die Türe füllt

dunkel wie der Grund einer Kamee,
die ein Schimmern durchläßt durch die Ränder;
und du meinst der Abend war nicht, ehe
sie heraustrat, um auf das Geländer

noch ein wenig von sich fortzulegen,
noch die Hände,—um ganz leicht zu sein:
wie dem Himmel von den Häuserreihn
hingereicht, von allem zu bewegen.

Lady on a Balcony

Suddenly she steps, wrapped into the wind,
brightly into brightness, as if singled out,
while now the room as if cut to fit
fills the door behind her

darkly like the background of a cameo,
and lets a glimmer through around its edges;
and you think the evening hadn't come
until she stepped out, and on the railing

set forth just a little of herself,
just her hands, —to be completely light:
as if passed on by the rows of houses
to the heavens, to be swayed by everything.

Begegnung in der Kastanien-Allee

Ihm ward des Eingangs grüne Dunkelheit
kühl wie ein Seidenmantel umgegeben
den er noch nahm und ordnete: als eben
am andern transparenten Ende, weit,

aus grüner Sonne, wie aus grünen Scheiben,
weiß eine einzelne Gestalt
aufleuchtete, um lange fern zu bleiben
und schließlich, von dem Lichterniedertreiben
bei jedem Schritte überwallt,

ein helles Wechseln auf sich herzutragen,
das scheu im Blond nach hinten lief.
Aber auf einmal war der Schatten tief,
und nahe Augen lagen aufgeschlagen

in einem neuen deutlichen Gesicht,
das wie in einem Bildnis verweilte
in dem Moment, da man sich wieder teilte:
erst war es immer, und dann war es nicht.

Encounter in the Chestnut Avenue

He felt the entrance's green darkness
wrapped coolly round him like a silken cloak
that he was still accepting and arranging;
when at the opposite transparent end, far off,

through green sunlight, as through green windowpanes,
whitely a solitary shape
flared up, long remaining distant
and then finally, the downdriving light
boiling over it at every step,

bearing on itself a bright pulsation,
which in the blond ran shyly to the back.
But suddenly the shade was deep,
and nearby eyes lay gazing

from a clear new unselfconscious face,
which, as in a portrait, lived intensely
in the instant things split off again:
first there forever, and then not at all.

Die Schwestern

Sieh, wie sie dieselben Möglichkeiten
anders an sich tragen und verstehn,
so als sähe man verschiedne Zeiten
durch zwei gleiche Zimmer gehn.

Jede meint die andere zu stützen,
während sie doch müde an ihr ruht;
und sie können nicht einander nützen,
denn sie legen Blut auf Blut,

wenn sie sich wie früher sanft berühren
und versuchen, die Allee entlang
sich geführt zu fühlen und zu führen:
Ach, sie haben nicht denselben Gang.

The Sisters

Look how the same possibilities
unfold in their opposite demeanors,
as though one saw different ages
passing through two identical rooms.

Each thinks that she props up the other,
while resting wearily on her support;
and they can't make use of one another,
for they cause blood to rest on blood,

when as in former times they softly touch
and try, along the tree-lined walks,
to feel themselves conducted and to lead;
ah, the ways they go are not the same.

Übung am Klavier

Der Sommer summt. Der Nachmittag macht müde;
sie atmete verwirrt ihr frisches Kleid
und legte in die triftige Etüde
die Ungeduld nach einer Wirklichkeit,

die kommen konnte: morgen, heute abend—,
die vielleicht da war, die man nur verbarg;
und vor den Fenstern, hoch und alles habend,
empfand sie plötzlich den verwöhnten Park.

Da brach sie ab; schaute hinaus, verschränkte
die Hände; wünschte sich ein langes Buch—
und schob auf einmal den Jasmingeruch
erzürnt zurück. Sie fand, daß er sie kränkte.

Piano Practice

The summer hums. The afternoon fatigues;
she breathed her crisp white dress distractedly
and put into that convincing étude
her impatience for a reality

that could come: tomorrow, this evening—,
that perhaps was there, was just kept hidden;
and at the window, tall and having everything,
she suddenly could feel the pampered park.

With that she broke off; gazed outside, locked
her hands together; wished for a long book—
and in a burst of anger shoved back
the jasmine scent. She found it made her sick.

Die Liebende

Das ist mein Fenster. Eben
bin ich so sanft erwacht.
Ich dachte, ich würde schweben.
Bis wohin reicht mein Leben,
und wo beginnt die Nacht?

Ich könnte meinen, alles
wäre noch Ich ringsum;
durchsichtig wie eines Kristalles
Tiefe, verdunkelt, stumm.

Ich könnte auch noch die Sterne
fassen in mir; so groß
scheint mir mein Herz; so gerne
ließ es ihn wieder los

den ich vielleicht zu lieben,
vielleicht zu halten begann.
Fremd, wie niebeschrieben
sieht mich mein Schicksal an.

Was bin ich unter diese
Unendlichkeit gelegt,
duftend wie eine Wiese,
hin und her bewegt,

rufend zugleich und bange,
daß einer den Ruf vernimmt,
und zum Untergange
in einem Andern bestimmt.

Woman in Love

That is my window. Just now
I have so softly wakened.
I thought that I would float.
How far does my life reach,
and where does the night begin?

I could think that everything
was still me all around;
transparent like a crystal's
depths, darkened, mute.

I could keep even the stars
within me; so immense
my heart seems to me; so willingly
it let him go again

whom I began perhaps
to love, perhaps to hold.
Like something strange, undreamt-of,
my fate now gazes at me.

For what, then, am I stretched out
beneath this endlessness,
exuding fragrance like a meadow,
swayed this way and that,

calling out and frightened
that someone will hear the call,
and destined to disappear
inside some other life.

Das Rosen-Innere

Wo ist zu diesem Innen
ein Außen? Auf welches Weh
legt man solches Linnen?
Welche Himmel spiegeln sich drinnen
in dem Binnensee
dieser offenen Rosen,
dieser sorglosen, sieh:
wie sie lose im Losen
liegen, als könnte nie
eine zitternde Hand sie verschütten.
Sie können sich selber kaum
halten; viele ließen
sich überfüllen und fließen
über von Innenraum
in die Tage, die immer
voller und voller sich schließen,
bis der ganze Sommer ein Zimmer
wird, ein Zimmer in einem Traum.

The Rose-Interior

Where for this Inside is there
an Outside? Upon what pain
is such linen placed?
What skies find themselves reflected
in the inland lake
of these open roses,
these carefree ones, look:
how loosely in the looseness
they relax, as though no trembling hand
could ever spill them.
They scarcely can contain
themselves; many let themselves
fill up with inner space
until they overflow and stream
into the days, which keep on
closing fuller and fuller,
until all of summer becomes
a room, a room within a dream.

Damen-Bildnis aus den
Achtziger-Jahren

Wartend stand sie an den schwergerafften
dunklen Atlasdraperien,
die ein Aufwand falscher Leidenschaften
über ihr zu ballen schien;

seit den noch so nahen Mädchenjahren
wie mit einer anderen vertauscht:
müde unter den getürmten Haaren,
in den Rüschen-Roben unerfahren
und von allen Falten wie belauscht

bei dem Heimweh und dem schwachen Planen,
wie das Leben weiter werden soll:
anders, wirklicher, wie in Romanen,
hingerissen und verhängnisvoll,—

daß man etwas erst in die Schatullen
legen dürfte, um sich im Geruch
von Erinnerungen einzulullen;
daß man endlich in dem Tagebuch

einen Anfang fände, der nicht schon
unterm Schreiben sinnlos wird und Lüge,
und ein Blatt von einer Rose trüge
in dem schweren leeren Medaillon,

welches liegt auf jedem Atemzug.
Daß man einmal durch das Fenster winkte;
diese schlanke Hand, die neuberingte,
hätte dran für Monate genug.

Lady's Portrait from the Eighties

Waiting she stood against the dark folds
of the densely gathered satin drapery,
which a grand display of false passions
seemed to clench into a knot above her;

ever since her childhood years, still so close,
standing as if in someone else's place;
weary beneath the piled-up hair,
inexperienced in the ruche-trimmed gown
and by all the folds as if eavesdropped on

amid the homesickness and the weak plans
for how life later on should be:
different, more real, the way it is in novels,
full of rapture and impending doom,—

so that one might first put something
inside one's jewel-casket, to lull oneself
in the odor of reminiscences;
so that one would find at last in one's diary

a beginning that does not become
meaningless and all lies in the writing;
and would carry the petal of a rose
inside the heavy empty locket

that weighs down every breath.
So that once one waved through the window;
this slender hand, newly ringed,
would be content with that for months.

Dame vor dem Spiegel

Wie in einem Schlaftrunk Spezerein
löst sie leise in dem flüssigklaren
Spiegel ihr ermüdetes Gebaren;
und sie tut ihr Lächeln ganz hinein.

Und sie wartet, daß die Flüssigkeit
davon steigt; dann gießt sie ihre Haare
in den Spiegel und, die wunderbare
Schulter hebend aus dem Abendkleid,

trinkt sie still aus ihrem Bild. Sie trinkt,
was ein Liebender im Taumel tränke,
prüfend, voller Mißtraun; und sie winkt

erst der Zofe, wenn sie auf dem Grunde
ihres Spiegels Lichter findet, Schränke
und das Trübe einer späten Stunde.

Lady at a Mirror

As in a sleeping-drink spices
softly she loosens in the liquid-clear
mirror her fatigued demeanor;
and she puts her smile deep inside.

And she waits while the liquid
rises from it; then she pours her hair
into the mirror, and, lifting one
wondrous shoulder from the evening gown,

she drinks quietly from her image. She drinks
what a lover would drink feeling dazed,
searching it, full of mistrust; and she only

beckons to her maid when at the bottom
of her mirror she finds candles, wardrobes,
and the cloudy dregs of a late hour.

Die Greisin

Weisse Freundinnen mitten im Heute
lachen und horchen und planen für morgen;
abseits erwägen gelassene Leute
langsam ihre besonderen Sorgen,

das Warum und das Wann und das Wie,
und man hört sie sagen: Ich glaube—;
aber in ihrer Spitzenhaube
ist sie sicher, als wüßte sie,

daß sie sich irren, diese und alle.
Und das Kinn, im Niederfalle,
lehnt sich an die weiße Koralle,
die den Schal zur Stirne stimmt.

Einmal aber, bei einem Gelache,
holt sie aus springenden Lidern zwei wache
Blicke und zeigt diese harte Sache,
wie man aus einem geheimen Fache
schöne ererbte Steine nimmt.

The Old Lady

Friends in white in the middle of today
laugh and eavesdrop and plan for tomorrow;
off in the margins self-composed people
slowly weigh their particular cares,

the Why and the When and the How,
and one hears them say: I believe—;
but in her lace cap she is all
sureness, as if she knew

that they were wrong, these and everyone.
And her chin, gently settling,
props itself against the white coral
that harmonizes shawl and brow.

Once, though, hearing superficial laughter,
she fetches from behind springing lids
two wakeful looks and shows this hardness,
the way one from a secret compartment
takes beautiful inherited gems.

Das Bett

Lass sie meinen, daß sich in privater
Wehmut löst, was einer dort bestritt.
Nirgend sonst als da ist ein Theater;
reiß den hohen Vorhang fort—: da tritt

vor den Chor der Nächte, der begann
ein unendlich breites Lied zu sagen,
jene Stunde auf, bei der sie lagen,
und zerreißt ihr Kleid und klagt sich an,

um der andern, um der Stunde willen,
die sich wehrt und wälzt im Hintergrunde;
denn sie konnte sie mit sich nicht stillen.
Aber da sie zu der fremden Stunde

sich gebeugt: da war auf ihr,
was sie am Geliebten einst gefunden,
nur so drohend und so groß verbunden
und entzogen wie in einem Tier.

The Bed

Let them suppose that in private sorrow
what one disputed there resolves and fades.
Nowhere else but there is a theater;
rip the high curtain back—: there stepped

before the chorus of the nights, which began
to say an endlessly extended song,
that hour with whom they lay,
and tears her garment and indicts herself,

for that other's, for that hour's sake
who writhes and defends herself in the background;
for she couldn't quiet her with herself.
But when she leaned across

to that remote hour: there was on her
what she by the loved one once had found,
only so threatening and so greatly united
and withdrawn the way it is in beasts.

Der Fremde

Ohne Sorgfalt, was die Nächsten dächten,
die er müde nichtmehr fragen hieß,
ging er wieder fort; verlor, verließ—.
Denn er hing an solchen Reisenächten

anders als an jeder Liebesnacht.
Wunderbare hatte er durchwacht,
die mit starken Sternen überzogen
enge Fernen auseinanderbogen
und sich wandelten wie eine Schlacht;

andre, die mit in den Mond gestreuten
Dörfern, wie mit hingehaltnen Beuten,
sich ergaben, oder durch geschonte
Parke graue Edelsitze zeigten,
die er gerne in dem hingeneigten
Haupte einen Augenblick bewohnte,
tiefer wissend, daß man nirgends bleibt;
und schon sah er bei dem nächsten Biegen
wieder Wege, Brücken, Länder liegen
bis an Städte, die man übertreibt.

Und dies alles immer unbegehrend
hinzulassen, schien ihm mehr als seines
Lebens Lust, Besitz und Ruhm.
Doch auf fremden Plätzen war ihm eines
täglich ausgetretnen Brunnensteines
Mulde manchmal wie ein Eigentum.

The Stranger

Neglecting what those nearest him would think,
all their questions wearily protesting,
he went away once more; let go, forgot—.
For he clung to such nights of travel

differently than to any night of love.
He had watched alert through wondrous ones,
which blanketed with strong stars
bent narrow distances apart
and kept on changing like a battle;

other ones, those with villages scattered
in the moonlight, as if with held-out booty,
surrendered, or else through well-kept
parks showed gray ancestral mansions,
which he gladly in his outstretched head
moved into for a moment, knowing
more deeply that nowhere does one remain;
and already around the next curve saw
roads again, bridges, landscapes reaching out
to cities which the mind magnifies.

And to let all this slip past without
desiring it, seemed more to him than his
life's pleasure, property, and fame.
Although in foreign squares the hollow
of a well-stone worn down day by day
was at times to him like something owned.

Die Anfahrt

War in des Wagens Wendung dieser Schwung?
War er im Blick, mit dem man die barocken
Engelfiguren, die bei blauen Glocken
im Felde standen voll Erinnerung,

annahm und hielt und wieder ließ, bevor
der Schloßpark schließend um die Fahrt sich drängte,
an die er streifte, die er überhängte
und plötzlich freigab: denn da war das Tor,

das nun, als hätte es sie angerufen,
die lange Front zu einer Schwenkung zwang,
nach der sie stand. Aufglänzend ging ein Gleiten

die Glastür abwärts; und ein Windhund drang
aus ihrem Aufgehn, seine nahen Seiten
heruntertragend von den flachen Stufen.

The Arrival

Did the coach's turn release this surge?
Was it in the glance with which those baroque
stone angels, standing full of memory
among bluebells in the open field,

were caught and held and dropped again, before
the castle park closed in around the ride,
which it brushed against, which it overhung
and suddenly set free: for there was the gate,

which now, as if it had shouted to it,
forced the long front into a curving round
after which it stood. A glide slipped gleaming

down the glass door; and from its opening
a greyhound pushed through, bearing its thin flanks
down shallow steps into the scene below.

Die Sonnenuhr

Selten reicht ein Schauer feuchter Fäule
aus dem Gartenschatten, wo einander
Tropfen fallen hören und ein Wander-
vogel lautet, zu der Säule,
die in Majoran und Koriander
steht und Sommerstunden zeigt;

nur sobald die Dame (der ein Diener
nachfolgt) in dem hellen Florentiner
über ihren Rand sich neigt,
wird sie schattig und verschweigt—.

Oder wenn ein sommerlicher Regen
aufkommt aus dem wogenden Bewegen
hoher Kronen, hat sie eine Pause;
denn sie weiß die Zeit nicht auszudrücken,
die dann in den Frucht- und Blumenstücken
plötzlich glüht im weißen Gartenhause.

The Sundial

Seldom does a shudder of damp decay
reach from the garden shadows, where drops
hear one another fall and a migratory
bird makes sounds, to the column,
which stands in marjoram and coriander
and shows the summer hours;

only when the lady (whom a servant
follows) in the bright wide-brimmed bonnet
bends down above its edge
does it grow shadowy and secretive—.

Or when a summer rain comes down
from the surging movements
of high treetops, does it pause;
for it can't express the kind of time
which then in the still-life fruits and flowers
suddenly sets the white gardenhouse aglow.

Schlaf-Mohn

Abseits im Garten blüht der böse Schlaf,
in welchem die, die heimlich eingedrungen,
die Liebe fanden junger Spiegelungen,
die willig waren, offen und konkav,

und Träume, die mit aufgeregten Masken
auftraten, riesiger durch die Kothurne—:
das alles stockt in diesen oben flasken
weichlichen Stengeln, die die Samenurne

(nachdem sie lang, die Knospe abwärts tragend,
zu welken meinten) festverschlossen heben:
gefranste Kelche auseinanderschlagend,
die fieberhaft das Mohngefäß umgeben.

Opium Poppy

Apart in the garden blooms the evil sleep,
in which those who have secretly entered
found the love of young mirror-images,
that were willing, open, and concave;

and dreams, that stepped out with excited masks,
striding more colossal in the buskin—:
all this thickens in these topmost slender
indolent stems, which (after thinking

for so long, their buds borne downward,
that they were fading) lift the tight-shut
seed-urns: flinging open frayed calyxes
that feverishly surround the poppy-cup.

Die Flamingos

Jardin des Plantes, Paris

In Spiegelbildern wie von Fragonard
ist doch von ihrem Weiß und ihrer Röte
nicht mehr gegeben, als dir einer böte,
wenn er von seiner Freundin sagt: sie war

noch sanft von Schlaf. Denn steigen sie ins Grüne
und stehn, auf rosa Stielen leicht gedreht,
beisammen, blühen, wie in einem Beet,
verführen sie verführender als Phryne

sich selber; bis sie ihres Auges Bleiche
hinhalsend bergen in der eignen Weiche,
in welcher Schwarz und Fruchtrot sich versteckt.

Auf einmal kreischt ein Neid durch die Volière;
sie aber haben sich erstaunt gestreckt
und schreiten einzeln ins Imaginäre.

The Flamingos

Jardin des Plantes, Paris

In mirrored images like Fragonard's
no more of their white and their red
is given, than someone would offer you
if he says of his mistress: she was still

soft with sleep. For when they rise into the greenness
and stand there, lightly twisted on pink stems,
together, blooming, as in some garden-plot,
they seduce themselves, more alluringly

than Phryne; until their necks curl down and they
bury their pale eyes in their own softness,
where black and fruit-red lie concealed.

Suddenly an envy shrieks through the great cage;
but they have stretched out in astonishment
and stride, each alone, into the world of dreams.

l. 9, *Phryne*: Greek courtesan, famed for her beauty; she is supposed to have
modelled for the sculptor Praxiteles.

Persisches Heliotrop

Es könnte sein, daß dir der Rose Lob
zu laut erscheint für deine Freundin: Nimm
das schön gestickte Kraut und überstimm
mit dringend flüsterndem Heliotrop

den Bülbül, der an ihren Lieblingsplätzen
sie schreiend preist und sie nicht kennt.
Denn sieh: wie süße Worte nachts in Sätzen
beisammenstehn ganz dicht, durch nichts getrennt,
aus der Vokale wachem Violett
hindüftend durch das stille Himmelbett—:

so schließen sich vor dem gesteppten Laube
deutliche Sterne zu der seidnen Traube
und mischen, daß sie fast davon verschwimmt,
die Stille mit Vanille und mit Zimmt.

Persian Heliotrope

It could be that for you the rose's praise
seems too loud to suit your mistress: Take
the beautifully embroidered herb and outvie
with urgently whispering heliotrope

the bulbul, which among her favorite walks
extolls her loudly and doesn't know her.
For look: as sweet words at night in sentences
pull close together, refusing separation,
from the vowels' wakeful violet
perfuming through the silent four-poster—:

so standing out above the quilted leaves
clear stars close to form the silken cluster
and mix, so that it almost blurs,
the silence with cinnamon and vanilla.

l. 5, *bulbul*: the Persian nightingale.

Schlaflied

Einmal wenn ich dich verlier,
wirst du schlafen können, ohne
daß ich wie eine Lindenkrone
mich verflüstre über dir?

Ohne daß ich hier wache und
Worte, beinah wie Augenlider,
auf deine Brüste, auf deine Glieder
niederlege, auf deinen Mund.

Ohne daß ich dich verschließ
und dich allein mit Deinem lasse
wie einen Garten mit einer Masse
von Melissen und Stern-Anis.

Lullaby

Some day when I lose you,
will you still be able to sleep,
without me to whisper over you
like a crown of linden branches?

Without me to stay awake here
and put words, almost like eyelids,
on your breasts, on your limbs,
down upon your mouth.

Without me to lock you up
and leave you alone with what is yours
like a garden thickly sown
with mint-balm and star-anise.

Der Pavillon

Aber selbst noch durch die Flügeltüren
mit dem grünen regentrüben Glas
ist ein Spiegeln lächelnder Allüren
und ein Glanz von jenem Glück zu spüren,
das sich dort, wohin sie nicht mehr führen,
einst verbarg, verklärte und vergaß.

Aber selbst noch in den Stein-Guirlanden
über der nicht mehr berührten Tür
ist ein Hang zur Heimlichkeit vorhanden
und ein stilles Mitgefühl dafür—,

und sie schauern manchmal, wie gespiegelt,
wenn ein Wind sie schattig überlief;
auch das Wappen, wie auf einem Brief
viel zu glücklich, überstürzt gesiegelt,

redet noch. Wie wenig man verscheuchte:
alles weiß noch, weint noch, tut noch weh—.
Und im Fortgehn durch die tränenfeuchte
abgelegene Allee

fühlt man lang noch auf dem Rand des Dachs
jene Urnen stehen, kalt, zerspalten:
doch entschlossen, noch zusammzuhalten
um die Asche alter Achs.

The Pavilion

But even now beyond the folding doors
with their green, rain-dim sheets of glass
a glint of beckoning caprice survives,
and a gleam from that happiness which once,
in a spot they've ceased to open on,
hid away, became transfigured, and forgot.

But even now in the stone festoon
above the door that's never any longer touched,
a tendency toward secretness persists,
and a silent sympathy for it—,

and they shudder sometimes, as if mirrored,
when a wind runs through them like a shadow;
even the coat of arms, as upon a letter
all too happily, overhastily sealed,

still speaks. How little has been driven off:
everything still knows, still weeps, still causes pain—.
And as you walk away through the tear-damp
unfrequented avenue

for a long time you feel on the roof's ledge
those urns standing there, cold and split apart:
yet determined still to hold together
around the ashes of old aches.

Die Entführung

Oft war sie als Kind ihren Dienerinnen
entwichen, um die Nacht und den Wind
(weil sie drinnen so anders sind)
draußen zu sehn an ihrem Beginnen;

doch keine Sturmnacht hatte gewiß
den riesigen Park so in Stücke gerissen,
wie ihn jetzt ihr Gewissen zerriß,

da er sie nahm von der seidenen Leiter
und sie weitertrug, weiter, weiter . . . :

bis der Wagen alles war.

Und sie roch ihn, den schwarzen Wagen,
um den verhalten das Jagen stand
und die Gefahr.
Und sie fand ihn mit Kaltem ausgeschlagen;
und das Schwarze und Kalte war auch in ihr.
Sie kroch in ihren Mantelkragen
und befühlte ihr Haar, als bliebe es hier,
und hörte fremd einen Fremden sagen:
Ichbinbeidir.

The Abduction

Often as a child she had run away
from her maids, to see the night and the wind
(since inside they are so different)
outside, at their beginnings;

yet surely no storm-filled night
had ever ripped that giant park to pieces
the way now her conscience tore it,

as he took her from the silken ladder
and bore her out beyond, farther, farther . . . :

until the carriage was all there was.

And she smelled it, that black carriage,
around which pursuit and danger
stood tensely held in check.
And she found it lined with cold;
and the black and cold was also in her.
She crept back into her hooded cape
and touched her hair, as if bidding it farewell,
and heard strangely a stranger say:
I'mherewithyou.

Rosa Hortensie

Wer nahm das Rosa an? Wer wußte auch,
daß es sich sammelte in diesen Dolden?
Wie Dinge unter Gold, die sich entgolden,
entröten sie sich sanft, wie im Gebrauch.

Daß sie für solches Rosa nichts verlangen.
Bleibt es für sie und lächelt aus der Luft?
Sind Engel da, es zärtlich zu empfangen,
wenn es vergeht, großmütig wie ein Duft?

Oder vielleicht auch geben sie es preis,
damit es nie erführe vom Verblühn.
Doch unter diesem Rosa hat ein Grün
gehorcht, das jetzt verwelkt und alles weiß.

Pink Hydrangea

Who would conceive this pink? And who would know
that it collected in these umbels?
Like things beneath gold, that shed their goldness,
they gently lose their red, as if from use.

That for such pink they demand nothing.
Does it stay for them and smile from the air?
Are angels there to take it tenderly
when it expires, unselfish like a scent?

Or perhaps they even relinquish it,
that it might never learn of blossoms fading.
Yet underneath this pink a green has
listened, which wilts now and knows everything.

Das Wappen

Wie ein Spiegel, der, von ferne tragend,
lautlos in sich aufnahm, ist der Schild;
offen einstens, dann zusammenschlagend
über einem Spiegelbild

jener Wesen, die in des Geschlechts
Weiten wohnen, nicht mehr zu bestreiten,
seiner Dinge, seiner Wirklichkeiten
(rechte links und linke rechts),

die er eingesteht und sagt und zeigt.
Drauf, mit Ruhm und Dunkel ausgeschlagen,
ruht der Spangenhelm, verkürzt,

den das Flügelkleinod übersteigt,
während seine Decke, wie mit Klagen,
reich und aufgeregt herniederstürzt.

The Coat of Arms

The shield is like a mirror, which draws things in
from far away and soundlessly absorbs them:
open for a time, then folding shut
over a mirror-image of

those beings, that live within the noble line's
deep spaces, no longer to be challenged,
of its objects, its realities
(right on left and left on right),

which it admits to and speaks of and displays.
Atop it, lined with fame and darkness,
rests the visored helm, indrawn,

which the winged crest triumphantly surmounts,
while its covering, as if with lament,
richly and turbulently spills down.

Der Junggeselle

Lampe auf den verlassenen Papieren,
und ringsum Nacht bis weit hinein ins Holz
der Schränke. Und er konnte sich verlieren
an sein Geschlecht, das nun mit ihm zerschmolz;
ihm schien, je mehr er las, er hätte ihren,
sie aber hatten alle seinen Stolz.

Hochmütig steiften sich die leeren Stühle
die Wand entlang, und lauter Selbstgefühle
machten sich schläfernd in den Möbeln breit;
von oben goß sich Nacht auf die Pendüle,
und zitternd rann aus ihrer goldnen Mühle,
ganz fein gemahlen, seine Zeit.

Er nahm sie nicht. Um fiebernd unter jenen,
als zöge er die Laken ihrer Leiber,
andere Zeiten wegzuzerrn.
Bis er ins Flüstern kam; (was war ihm fern?)
Er lobte einen dieser Briefeschreiber,
als sei der Brief an ihn: Wie du mich kennst;
und klopfte lustig auf die Seitenlehnen.
Der Spiegel aber, innen unbegrenzter,
ließ leise einen Vorhang aus, ein Fenster—:
denn dorten stand, fast fertig, das Gespenst.

The Bachelor

A lamp on the abandoned documents,
and night all around, reaching far inside
the wooden shelves. And he could lose himself
in his lineage, which now fused with him;
it seemed to him, the more he read, that he
possessed their pride, though all of them had his.

Haughtily the empty chairs stiffened up
along the wall, and pure self-esteems
stretched out drowsily in the furniture;
from above night poured on the antique clock,
and from its golden mill there streamed
tremblingly, and very finely ground, his time.

He left it there. And feverishly among *them*,
as if tugging at their bodies' shrouds,
tore other times away. Till he was
whispering; (what, for him, was distant?)
He praised one of these letter writers,
as if the letter were to him: How well you know me;
and slapped jovially on the chair's arms.
But the mirror, less limited within,
quietly released a curtain, a window—:
for there, almost ready, stood the specter.

Der Einsame

Nein: ein Turm soll sein aus meinem Herzen
und ich selbst an seinen Rand gestellt:
wo sonst nichts mehr ist, noch einmal Schmerzen
und Unsäglichkeit, noch einmal Welt.

Noch ein Ding allein im Übergroßen,
welches dunkel wird und wieder licht,
noch ein letztes, sehnendes Gesicht
in das Nie-zu-Stillende verstoßen,

noch ein äußerstes Gesicht aus Stein,
willig seinen inneren Gewichten,
das die Weiten, die es still vernichten,
zwingen, immer seliger zu sein.

The Solitary

No: a tower shall rise out of my heart,
and I myself will be placed at its edge;
where nothing else exists, once again pain
and unsayableness, once again world.

Still one thing alone in immensity
growing dark and then light again,
still one last face full of longing
thrust out into the unappeasable,

still one uttermost face made of stone
heeding only its own inner gravity,
while the distances that silently destroy it
force it on to an ever deeper bliss.

Der Leser

Wer kennt ihn, diesen, welcher sein Gesicht
wegsenkte aus dem Sein zu einem zweiten,
das nur das schnelle Wenden voller Seiten
manchmal gewaltsam unterbricht?

Selbst seine Mutter wäre nicht gewiß,
ob *er* es ist, der da mit seinem Schatten
Getränktes liest. Und wir, die Stunden hatten,
was wissen wir, wieviel ihm hinschwand, bis

er mühsam aufsah: alles auf sich hebend,
was unten in dem Buche sich verhielt,
mit Augen, welche, statt zu nehmen, gebend
anstießen an die fertig-volle Welt:
wie stille Kinder, die allein gespielt,
auf einmal das Vorhandene erfahren;
doch seine Züge, die geordnet waren,
blieben für immer umgestellt.

The Reader

Who knows him, this youth who's let his face sink down
from his own existence to a second one,
which only the quick turning of full pages
sometimes violently interrupts?

Even his mother would not be sure
it's *he* who sits there reading something
saturated with his shadow. And we, who have hours,
how can we know how much of him was lost

before with effort he looked up: raising to himself
all that inhered in the book's depths,
with eyes which, instead of taking, bumped
givingly into the full-finished world:
the way quiet children, who have played alone,
suddenly experience what's at hand;
but his features, which were in order,
remained forever recomposed.

Der Apfelgarten

Borgeby-Gård

Komm gleich nach dem Sonnenuntergange,
sieh das Abendgrün des Rasengrunds;
ist es nicht, als hätten wir es lange
angesammelt und erspart in uns,

um es jetzt aus Fühlen und Erinnern,
neuer Hoffnung, halbvergeßnem Freun,
noch vermischt mit Dunkel aus dem Innern,
in Gedanken vor uns hinzustreun

unter Bäume wie von Dürer, die
das Gewicht von hundert Arbeitstagen
in den überfüllten Früchten tragen,
dienend, voll Geduld, versuchend, wie

das, was alle Maße übersteigt,
noch zu heben ist und hinzugeben,
wenn man willig, durch ein langes Leben
nur das Eine will und wächst und schweigt.

The Apple Orchard

Borgeby-Gård

Come just after sunset and behold it,
the evening greenness of the grassy earth;
is it not as if we had for ages
collected and saved it up inside us,

in order now from feeling and remembrance,
new hope, half-forgotten rejoicing,
still mingled with darkness from our depths,
to scatter it in thoughts before us

under trees as if by Dürer, which bear
the weight of a hundred days of labor
in the efflorescence of brimming fruit,
serving, full of patience, trying out

how that which goes beyond all measure
is still to be raised up and sacrificed,
when one willingly, throughout a long life,
wills just one thing and grows and holds one's peace.

Mohammeds Berufung

Da aber als in sein Versteck der Hohe,
sofort Erkennbare: der Engel, trat,
aufrecht, der lautere und lichterlohe:
da tat er allen Anspruch ab und bat

bleiben zu dürfen der von seinen Reisen
innen verwirrte Kaufmann, der er war;
er hatte nie gelesen—und nun gar
ein *solches* Wort, zu viel für einen Weisen.

Der Engel aber, herrisch, wies und wies
ihm, was geschrieben stand auf seinem Blatte,
und gab nicht nach und wollte wieder: *Lies.*

Da las er: so, daß sich der Engel bog.
Und war schon einer, der gelesen *hatte*
und konnte und gehorchte und vollzog.

Mohammed's Summoning

But then when the Angel—impossible
to mistake—stepped into his hiding-place,
erect, regal, all purity and blaze:
then he renounced all claims and begged

that he might go on being that merchant
all confused from his travels, which he was;
he had never learned to read—and now
such a word, too much even for a wise man.

But the Angel, imperious, showed and
showed him what was written on his page
and would not give way and once more willed: *Read.*

Then he read: so deeply, that the Angel bowed.
And was already someone who *had* read
and was able and obeyed and brought to pass.

Der Berg

Sechsunddreissig Mal und hundert Mal
hat der Maler jenen Berg geschrieben,
weggerissen, wieder hingetrieben
(sechsunddreißig Mal und hundert Mal)

zu dem unbegreiflichen Vulkane,
selig, voll Versuchung, ohne Rat,—
während der mit Umriß Angetane
seiner Herrlichkeit nicht Einhalt tat:

tausendmal aus allen Tagen tauchend,
Nächte ohne gleichen von sich ab
fallen lassend, alle wie zu knapp;
jedes Bild im Augenblick verbrauchend,
von Gestalt gesteigert zu Gestalt,
teilnahmslos und weit und ohne Meinung—,
um auf einmal wissend, wie Erscheinung,
sich zu heben hinter jedem Spalt.

The Mountain

Thirty-six and then a hundred times
the painter wrote that mountain,
torn away, always driven back again
(thirty-six and then a hundred times)

to the incomprehensible volcano,
blissful, wholly tempted, without a clue,—
while that enigma clothed in outline
held back nothing of its majesty;

a thousand times emerging from each day,
letting nights without equal
fall away, all as if too tight;
exhausting every image in an instant,
from shape mounting on to shape,
indifferent and distant and opinionless—,
only to abruptly grow all-knowing,
and rise up ghostlike behind each cleft.

The Japanese painter Hokusai (1760–1849) produced two series of colored
woodblock prints of scenes unified by the presence of the volcano Fujiyama:
Thirty-six Views of Mount Fuji: Southerly Wind and Fine Weather (in a broad-
sheet format), followed by *One Hundred Views of Mount Fuji* (in three bound
volumes).

Der Ball

Du Runder, der das Warme aus zwei Händen
im Fliegen, oben, fortgiebt, sorglos wie
sein Eigenes; was in den Gegenständen
nicht bleiben kann, zu unbeschwert für sie,

zu wenig Ding und doch noch Ding genug,
um nicht aus allem draußen Aufgereihten
unsichtbar plötzlich in uns einzugleiten:
das glitt in dich, du zwischen Fall und Flug

noch Unentschlossener: der, wenn er steigt,
als hätte er ihn mit hinaufgehoben,
den Wurf entführt und freiläßt—, und sich neigt
und einhält und den Spielenden von oben
auf einmal eine neue Stelle zeigt,
sie ordnend wie zu einer Tanzfigur,

um dann, erwartet und erwünscht von allen,
rasch, einfach, kunstlos, ganz Natur,
dem Becher hoher Hände zuzufallen.

The Ball

You round one, who take the warmth from two hands
and pass it on in flight, above, blithely
as if it were your own; what's too unburdened
to remain in objects, not thing enough

and yet sufficiently a thing so that
it doesn't slip from all the outer grids
and glide invisibly into our being:
it glided into you, you between fall and flight

still the undecided: who, when you rise,
as if you had drawn it up with you,
abduct and liberate the throw—, and bend
and pause and suddenly from above
show those playing a new place,
arranging them as for a dance's turn,

in order then, awaited and desired by all,
swift, simple, artless, completely nature,
to fall into the cup of upstretched hands.

Das Kind

Unwillkürlich sehn sie seinem Spiel
lange zu; zuweilen tritt das runde
seiende Gesicht aus dem Profil,
klar und ganz wie eine volle Stunde,

welche anhebt und zu Ende schlägt.
Doch die Andern zählen nicht die Schläge,
trüb von Mühsal und vom Leben träge;
und sie merken gar nicht, wie es trägt—,

wie es alles trägt, auch dann, noch immer,
wenn es müde in dem kleinen Kleid
neben ihnen wie im Wartezimmer
sitzt und warten will auf seine Zeit.

The Child

Without meaning to they stand watching
while it plays: occasionally the round
living face emerges from the profile,
clear and whole like some ripened hour

that rises up and chimes unto its end.
But the others don't keep track of the strokes,
dim from toil and sluggish from life;
and they don't even notice how it bears—,

how it bears everything, even then, still,
when wearily in its small clothes dressed up
beside them as if in the waiting room
it sits and keeps on waiting for its time.

Der Hund

Da oben wird das Bild von einer Welt
aus Blicken immerfort erneut und gilt.
Nur manchmal, heimlich, kommt ein Ding und stellt
sich neben ihn, wenn er durch dieses Bild

sich drängt, ganz unten, anders, wie er ist;
nicht ausgestoßen und nicht eingereiht,
und wie im Zweifel seine Wirklichkeit
weggebend an das Bild, das er vergißt,

um dennoch immer wieder sein Gesicht
hineinzuhalten, fast mit einem Flehen,
beinah begreifend, nah am Einverstehen
und doch verzichtend: denn er wäre nicht.

The Dog

Up there the image of a world is through
glances constantly subscribed to and renewed.
On occasion, secretly, a thing comes up
and stands beside him, when through that image

he pushes, down below, different, as he is;
not expelled and not assigned a place,
and giving away his reality as if in doubt
on the image that he forgets, only to

stick his face inside again and again,
almost with a pleading, on the verge
of comprehending, close to an agreement
and yet reneging: for he wouldn't be.

er Käferstein

Sind nicht Sterne fast in deiner Nähe
und was giebt es, das du nicht umspannst,
da du dieser harten Skarabäe
Karneolkern gar nicht fassen kannst

ohne jenen Raum, der ihre Schilder
niederhält, auf deinem ganzen Blut
mitzutragen; niemals war er milder,
näher, hingegebener. Er ruht

seit Jahrtausenden auf diesen Käfern,
wo ihn keiner braucht und unterbricht;
und die Käfer schließen sich und schläfern
unter seinem wiegenden Gewicht.

The Beetle-Stone

Are not stars almost within your reach
and what is there that you don't encompass,
since you cannot ever grasp these hard
scarabs' dense carnelian cores

without bearing too, on all your blood,
that space which holds their wing-shards down.
Never was space gentler, closer, more
self-surrendered. It has rested

for thousands of years upon these beetles,
where no one interrupts or uses it;
and the beetles fold in upon themselves
and sleep beneath its gently rocking weight.

Buddha in der Glorie

Mitte aller Mitten, Kern der Kerne,
Mandel, die sich einschließt und versüßt,—
dieses Alles bis an alle Sterne
ist dein Fruchtfleisch: Sei gegrüßt.

Sieh, du fühlst, wie nichts mehr an dir hängt;
im Unendlichen ist deine Schale,
und dort steht der starke Saft und drängt.
Und von außen hilft ihm ein Gestrahle,

denn ganz oben werden deine Sonnen
voll und glühend umgedreht.
Doch in dir ist schon begonnen,
was die Sonnen übersteht.

Buddha in Glory

Center of all centers, core of cores,
almond, that closes in and sweetens,—
this entire world out to all the stars
is your fruit-flesh: we greet you.

Look, you feel how nothing any longer
clings to you; your husk is in infinity,
and there the strong juice stands and presses.
And from outside a radiance assists it,

for high above, your suns in full splendor
have wheeled blazingly around.
Yet already there's begun inside you
what lasts beyond the suns.

Design by David Bullen
Typeset in Mergenthaler Fournier
by Wilsted & Taylor
Printed by Haddon Craftsmen
on acid-free paper